Donated to

St. Mary's Library

in memory of

 Gregory A. Young

WHAT
ABOUT
THE
CHILDREN?

A Divorced Parent's Handbook

WHAT ABOUT THE CHILDREN?

A Divorced Parent's Handbook

by *Francine Susan Spilke*

A HERBERT MICHELMAN BOOK

CROWN PUBLISHERS, INC.
New York

To Steven and Gary, my sons
To David, my husband

Special thanks are due to my publisher,
Herb Michelman, for his enthusiasm and
diligence in guiding the book to completion.

My gratitute also to my husband, David, whose
unfailing support, patience, and constant
encouragement were indispensable.

Printed in the United States of America

Published simultaneously in Canada by General Publishing Company Limited

Library of Congress Cataloging in Publication Data

Spilke, Francine Susan.
    What about the children?

    (Her The divorced family)
    Bibliography: p.
    1. Divorce—United States. 2. Children of divorced
parents—United States. 3. Divorcees—United States—
Family relationships. I. Title. II. Series.
HQ777.5.S64 1979   301.42'84'0973   79-9265
ISBN 0-517-53261-1

Contents

Introduction   vii

1   Accepting the Reality of Divorce: Adult Feelings   1
2   Telling Your Child You Are Getting Divorced   5
3   Accepting the Reality of Divorce: Children's Feelings   14
4   Separation vs. the Divorce   23
5   What Do I Tell My Friends and Relatives?   26
6   Grandparents   29
7   Deciding with Whom a Child Should Live   34
8   Moving Out and Other Changes (Relocating and Money
    Matters)   36
9   Visiting Days   40
10 Communicating with Your Child   45
11 Helping Children Cope with Their Feelings   48
12 The Working Mother   53
13 When Fathers Have Custody   55
14 Dating   57
15 Living with Someone to Whom You Are Not Married   59
16 The Joy of Remarriage   63
17 The Co-Parent (Stepparent)   66
18 How to Answer Your Child's Accusations   73
19 Special Problems   74

Alcoholism, Drug Addiction, Mental Illness	74
When a Judge Must Decide Custody	75
When Parents Continue to Disagree	75
A Parent Who Does Not Love a Child	76
Conclusion What Does It All Add Up To?	78
Epilogue	80
Bibliography	81

Introduction

Today, with one out of every two marriages destined to end in court, it is clear that divorce proceedings are becoming almost as common as wedding ceremonies.

Fortunately, in our enlightened society, the legal dissolution of an unsuccessful partnership between a man and a woman is no longer looked upon as shameful, sinful, or even necessarily tragic. Divorce no longer carries a stigma.

Rather, it is a logical step taken when people, after due consideration, decide that their marriages are too painful, unfulfilling, or unrewarding to merit continuation. Obviously, however, divorce may then prove one of life's most traumatic experiences for adults and children alike.

Divorce makes us all vulnerable to the same pitfalls. With the best of intentions, we as parents can find ourselves engaging in very destructive behavior. This book has been written to try to prevent children from becoming the victims of their parents' divorce. Many of the ways that parents conduct themselves unwittingly produce serious problems in the children.

Divorce *is* a highly emotionally charged event. Children cannot help but become the victims of a divorce when they are living with a negatively charged adult in a negatively charged environment.

No two people will react in the same way, nor face the same set of circumstances identically. Although most divorced people have certain similarities, there is a danger in overgeneralizing and underestimating the importance of the differences and uniqueness of each divorce situation.

It is with this in mind that this series of three books, *The Divorced Family,* has been written. Each of us is different, hence our reasons for divorce are different. I have attempted to isolate those elements that can be recognized in most divorce situations to offer a keener awareness and insight into the multitude of problems your divorce can create.

I would like to begin by introducing myself to you. There are many things that I am going to talk to you about that even your best friend would be wary of discussing with you. If you are to benefit from anything I have to say, it is important that you know my intentions and the background of reference from which I speak. My book is in no way intended to chastise or reprimand parents for behaving in some of the ways I am going to discuss in this book. Quite the contrary; my intention is to point out the quicksands into which we may sink, the vulnerabilities and weaknesses of all of us at the time of a divorce. Condemning ourselves for destructive behavior is beside the point. I hope to help you avoid problems, or to help you toward redesigned behavior if you and your children have already stumbled into them.

I believe that most parents earnestly try to do the best they can for their children and are most unhappy when they find they have failed. Intensifying that unhappiness is parents' not unusual discovery that they do not know how to cope with a situation that demands more knowledge and experience than they have.

If I can make you aware of the nature of the problems that some of you may already be facing and others of you may be about to face, I will have accomplished my goal.

Let me tell you briefly now about my own situation. At the time of my divorce I was thirty years old and had two boys aged three and five. My particular circumstances made it necessary for me to leave my home in New York and temporarily move in with my parents in Florida.

During the six months that I lived in Florida I organized discussion seminars for divorced parents and led these meetings on a weekly basis. I was asked for and found myself giving advice about problems many parents were having with their children, as well as with their own adjustment to their new divorced way of life. But even greater than the parent's need for help was the children's need. The opportunity to talk about their anger, hurt, anxiety, and feelings of guilt was, I think, helpful to many of them. I have tried in these pages to make what they taught me available to all parents.

Clouded by pain or anger or guilt but with the best of intentions, parents will approach their children in the belief that they are proffering help, when all they are really doing is giving the child a very biased, often bitter, and distorted account of what is going on. This is both unfair and unfortunate for the child and the parent. For children it is only creating more confusion and hurt in the long run. For parents it is a shedding of dignity and self-respect. The child begins to see the parents as bitter, angry persons and may even have doubts as to how truthful they are, often resulting in a lack of trust.

This book and my coordinated books for children, *What About Me?* and *The Family That Changed*, rest on three values. They are: courage, honesty, and parent-child communication.

I place courage as the first order of priority because without this it is difficult to be honest and practically impossible to have any meaningful communication with others, especially with one's children.

I have repeated to myself at some of the most difficult and trying moments in my own life, "Until the pain of the problem becomes greater than the pain of its solution you will not solve the problem." I believe this is the essence of what courage is all about. For it is often so much easier to live a life of despair and misery than it is to take the necessary steps that would resolve the conflicts. If we are to meet life head on and emerge whole human beings, it is necessary to face the reality of our own being. For many of us the most courageous feat of our life is that first step into our own mirror. Most of us who are involved in a divorce find that we have not stepped into our mirror painlessly, but have collided with it. The impact and the glass splinters can cut very deeply. If you are going to emerge as someone who will be useful to both yourself and your children you must muster all the courage you can. Courageous acts are roots from which you will grow.

The word "courage" is familiar enough to all of us but how does the word relate to us? What exactly do I mean by "courage" in this context? There is no definition that will apply to each and every one of us alike. But there are certain principles that we must all exercise in our own way. The will and ability to see and accept things the way they are is perhaps the backbone of courage. The rationalizations and defenses we use to protect ourselves from reality are instinctive for most of us. Generally we lack the real desire to confront those aspects of reality that do not please us. Sometimes it is easier to conceal and disguise our real motives than it is to meet them honestly.

But the essence of one's self-respect comes from our ability to cope with life and meet these challenges successfully. An individual who lacks self-respect has little to offer himself and consequently has little to offer others.

For many of us, divorce was the result of our accumulated failures. Some of our greatest self-growth emerges with the ability to recognize the failures of the past. To see ourselves realistically is a requisite first step.

Even under the most amiable circumstances, a divorce takes its toll on all who are involved. I have a very optimistic outlook on life and as such I can bring this same optimism to the circumstances surrounding a divorce. I would prefer to look upon a divorce as a chance for a new, hopefully happier, future. I refuse to accept a divorce as a setback in life, even if it may temporarily appear to be so. The optimistic approach is one that leaves you believing that when the storm is over and the troubled waters have receded, life will be even happier. For some this may sound like a child's fantasy. Others will recognize it as a positive attitude toward life.

Let me add a few words here for those of you who find it impossible to be optimistic about your future. I am in sympathy with and have compassion for the heartbreak and sorrow divorce causes most adults. I am also aware of the financial hardships and burdens that can occur. But I would caution anyone against allowing self-pity and remorse to dominate his or her life at this or any other time. Because the only chance you have for rebuilding a successful and happy life is to fight against adversity and feelings of loneliness and bitterness. The courage you must summon up for yourself extends far beyond the present. It is the foundation from which you must draw all your strength if you are to help your children through this very difficult period of adjustment.

This brings us to the next of my values, *honesty*. Without being honest with yourself, it is impossible to be honest with your children. Whatever pattern you establish now, be it truthfulness or deceitfulness, it will remain with you in the years to come. You cannot nullify the reality of a divorce by camouflaging its existence. The falsehoods you tell now will affect your children all their lives.

Short of cruelty, there is no shame in anything one does with one's life as long as it is done with honesty and forethought. The attitudes displayed by parents during the divorce will have much to do with how the divorce will affect the children.

But courage and honesty can only pave the way for the most important of all, *communication;* specifically *parent-child communication.*

Communication is one of the most valued factors that enables human beings to survive as a species. The ultimate dream of world peace rests upon the human race's ability to communicate ideas. There is little in our normal daily lives that is not dependent on our ability to communicate ideas, feelings, happenings, discoveries. But how successful is communication among people? Often feelings, moods, and emotions cannot be expressed in words alone but must be revealed more subtly by gesture, tone, glance. Our feelings and emotions are often the most sadly neglected and abused aspect of our relationship with others. For many of us there is no time to indulge in emotions or to acknowledge our feelings and sentiments. And by denying ourselves the right to experience the joy of our own feelings, we can rob ourselves of the essence of being human.

Parents have the opportunity to experience one of the most beautiful and fulfilling human relationships by encouraging children to discuss everything openly. Parents must teach children to express their feelings without fear. A kind, understanding parent will provide a child the incentive to talk about the things that are troublesome. Honesty is the keynote to this relationship if a child is to have confidence in the parent. Especially during the time of a divorce, the atmosphere must be one of trust and tolerance. The fears and uncertainties a child has are greatly compounded by well-meaning adults trying to conceal the truth. It is always easier to cope with a problem when you know the facts. Children worry more about the things they are not told than about information offered forthright. A child's imagination can create problems far worse than the actual problems. The only way children can come to terms with their parents' divorce is by learning to accept the divorce as a reality.

At best, divorce is difficult for children to understand. If they are to cope, however, with the hurt and disappointments, children need the support of both parents. If this is not possible, surely they must be able to rely upon one parent for strength and encouragement as well as love and understanding. This is a vital ingredient of parent-child communication.

Some children are unnecessarily victimized by divorce. I hope that this book will help parents understand the child's predicament so that they will be able to explain the situation properly and avoid disturbing the child excessively. Children will have greater respect for parents who have respect for them.

Many adults often underestimate a child's intelligence and instincts. Most children are capable of understanding far more than parents give them credit for. Some parents are at a loss to explain certain things to their children. We have all been in this situation. We mean well, but with the best of intentions we simply do not know what to say. Indeed, some parents avoid the real issues and this only confuses the child even more. In the accompanying books for children I have attempted to tell the children what is really happening so that they will be better able to understand and, we hope, assuage many of their fears. Parents will find it helpful to use these children's books as a guide to explaining many of the things that may be troubling either the parent or the child.

There are many times when parents are not aware of how their actions affect a child. The children's books encourage children to point out to the parent things that are particularly disturbing to them. This is not meant to encourage children to be intolerant or disrespectful to their elders.

The suggestions should help alleviate some of the tension and anxiety that can burden a child who is not given the opportunity to express them. But this technique will be productive and successful only if there is a warm foundation of parent-child communication and a relationship that is loving and free.

The children's books strongly encourage a child to talk to each of the parents about what he or she has read. The books will create new awareness for many children, giving them much to think about and digest. Your help will be needed if the child is to understand what he or she has read. It will work best if you encourage open discussions about each subject.

How much your child will be helped will depend greatly upon your attitude as well as your discussions. The benefits that parent and child will derive from learning to communicate frankly and honestly with each other are huge. I can only urge each of you to listen to what your child is saying. Get to know your child. Let your child get to know *you*.

Before giving *What About Me?* or *The Family That Changed* to your child, read the entire book. You will be better prepared for his or her questions. Read the first chapter of *What About Me?* together with your child to encourage positive acceptance of the book and to commence an open discussion about the subjects in it.

Should an older child not want you to read along, respect that preference, but with the assurance that you will be available to discuss any questions. Therefore, when you give the child the book, remain in the house. You will find, I trust, a new, more mature relationship with your child.

WHAT
ABOUT
THE
CHILDREN?

A Divorced Parent's Handbook

1

Accepting the Reality of Divorce: Adult Feelings

Some people are more successful than others at coping with the stresses of a divorce. Accepting your divorce is something you must do for yourself, just as you must learn to build a new life yourself.

Depending upon the circumstances that caused the divorce, many parents emerge with a negative attitude. The rejected and lonely husband or wife is scarcely the ideal parent for a child to be living with. There is very little anyone can do to eliminate the void of loneliness that a newly divorced person often feels. For those of you who are at this point of despair perhaps it will be of some comfort to know that you are not alone. Almost every person who goes through with a divorce will be subject to a similar experience at one time or another. The differences will be in the extent to which each of us allows our disappointment or despair to dominate our lives. This is very similar to the period of mourning someone goes through after the death of a loved one. It is not easy to overcome loneliness and believe there is, at a time like this, a brighter tomorrow. But if you begin to allow the hurt and bitterness you are feeling to dominate your personality, it will affect all your activities and relationships. People will find you difficult to be with and, worst of all, your children will find it very difficult to live with you. Your constant unhappiness will create tension and anxiety in your home and breed nothing but unhappiness for everyone.

Your attitude after the divorce can be influenced by the circumstances that caused it. Do not try to wage a one person war against the entire male or female population. You cannot "get even" with all men or women because things did not work out with your ex-spouse. You cannot rebuild your own ego by downgrading someone else. How one goes about rebuilding an ego is not within the purview of this book. The concern here is with the adverse effect an emotionally distraught parent has upon a child's development. However difficult, you must consider the effects of your state of mind on your children. Remember, no matter what you are going through, they too miss someone they love and must now learn to live with only one parent at a time.

Prolonged depression may indicate that you need outside help. There are many clinics and counseling centers that now have specialists who are trained to work with divorce situations. These professionals have been trained to help you through this period of adjustment. Do not be ashamed to seek help if you need it. You cannot possibly attempt to help your children overcome their angry and bitter feelings unless you can learn to cope with your own.

In addition to professional help, there are many organizations that have been formed specifically to meet the needs of divorced parents. Most major cities have chapters of "Parents Without Partners" and most health centers and local Ys today hold single parent seminars. Adult education programs now frequently include an evening course for the single parent. And many social groups have been organized for the purpose of helping single parents meet each other. Take advantage of these groups and become a joiner.

In *What About Me?*, I have tried to give children a realistic idea of the ups and downs of living with one parent at a time. It is important that children understand that this new way of living is as different for you as for them. I have stressed the need for cooperation and consideration and that they try to understand that their parents also have problems. Although this places great responsibility upon the child, the real responsibility still lies with the parent.

Awareness of your behavior toward your children is very important. Children cannot solve adult problems. A parent who leans on a child and consults him or her on all decisions is placing too much responsibility on the child. Although they may appear to relish the independence and control they are given, too much autonomy and responsibility can make a child insecure. Children still need to know that they can rely on their parents for guidance and control during their period of growth and development. They need to know that, regardless of any other family problems, their parents are capable of asserting good judgment and making the proper decisions regarding the children. Children want direction from their parents and need to see that in spite of the divorce they are still subject to the necessary direction. Parents who let their children become the decision makers are doing them a grave disservice in another way. These children often find it more difficult to cope in later adult relationships.

Some parents feel divorce brands them with a scarlet letter. If this ever were the case, it is no longer true. No one enters a marriage with the intention of getting a divorce. But it is better to dissolve a bad marriage than to continue to live unhappily ever after. The issue of who is to blame is academic. It may help to know that as many troubled children come from two-parent homes as from broken homes. A divorced parent can still be a good parent. A sensitive concerned parent is at hand, when he or she is needed. Being divorced should not prevent this. A parent's perceptiveness and responsiveness to a child's needs are the mark of a good parent.

Parents are far from perfect people, divorced or together. Yet many of them try to convince their children otherwise. The myth of the all-knowing parent is still being perpetuated. When children eventually discover that their parents are as vulnerable as most other people, they are terribly disappointed. And children whose parents are being divorced simply learn at a much earlier age that their parents are not infallible.

One of the most common problems many parents share is that of parental guilt over what the divorce will do to the children. The guilt that parents feel over their divorce can often cause a parent to indulge a child much to the detriment of both the child and the parent. Filling the house with expensive clothes or toys cannot buy back a child's love or compensate for being an inadequate single parent. It is very important that parents come to terms with their own guilt and not allow an unrealistic burden to dominate their behavior. Being aware that these feelings exist is the first step to overcoming them.

I do not believe in martyrdom—the devoted parent, so guilt ridden that he or she feels it necessary to sacrifice personal happiness "for the sake of the children." This syndrome is not restricted exclusively to divorced parents. It is to be seen as frequently among married parents. But the divorced parent becomes more susceptible to the feelings of guilt and overprotectiveness that give rise to this type of behavior. Rarely is it necessary for parents to sacrifice their own happiness for the sake of a child. Children are far more resilient than most parents realize. A happy, satisfied parent has a better chance of having a happy, satisfied child.

It is not unusual for a parent to harbor feelings of resentment toward the very child he or she is trying so hard to protect. This creates another kind of guilt. Parents with such feelings find themselves resenting the responsibility of having to raise children alone. They may have visions of

[3]

how uncomplicated and free their lives might be without children. Parents may reveal this unconscious resentment in outward behavior.

I mention this only to help a parent stop and think about his or her own feelings. A divorce need not be a catastrophic event. When parents can come to terms with themselves and their lives, they are better able to guide their children to maturity.

Both parents should be able to participate equally in the upbringing of the children. If discipline is to be effective, it is essential that the divorced parents honor one another's decisions. They must make a concerted effort to be consistent in the rules they set for the children. If one parent is permissive and the other strict, the child often winds up playing one parent against the other. This is true for families where there is no divorce. But it becomes even more confusing and disruptive for the child when a divorce has occurred. Because not only is the child's environment changing when he or she is with each parent but so is what is expected of him or her. This not only engenders additional antagonism between the parents, but can do great damage to the child. Children need consistent limits. A parent can be a friend to the child and still be able to command respect. This can be accomplished by being a parent first and a friend second.

In *What About Me?* there is a special section entitled "When Parents Use a Child for a Substitute." I am referring to a parent's use of a child as a replacement for the companion he or she no longer has in marriage.

Children can never replace an adult in a relationship. Parent-child relationships often deteriorate because a parent places a child in the role of a confidant. Mothers may tell their teen-age daughters all about their dates. Fathers may boast to their older sons about their sexual conquests. Parents may burden their older children with their loneliness and frustration. Most parents who are caught up in this role substitution may not realize it. If you are unsure of the attitudes and feelings you are projecting onto your children, it is wise to seek the advice of some other adult whose opinion you respect. Candid and full discussion—which I repeatedly urge in *What About Me?* and *The Family That Changed*—is equally essential for adults. But whereas a child's parent is almost invariably the best conversational partner, the parent's child is most unlikely to fill the reverse role adequately.

2

Telling Your Child You Are Getting Divorced

There is no "best" way for parents to tell children they are getting a divorce. But there are important guidelines you can follow.

To avoid the possibility that they may first hear the news from a relative or friend, you must be the one to break the news. A father, jogging with his twelve-year-old son, met a friend who had recently been divorced. She could hardly wait to tell him how sorry she was to hear that he too was getting divorced. She wanted to know when he planned to move out and if he had found an apartment yet. His son stood there stunned, hearing the traumatic news for the first time.

A five-year-old was asked by a friend at school, "I heard my mother say to my father that your parents were getting a divorce. Does that mean they will have to give you away?"

It is grossly unfair to expose children to incidents like this. Until the divorce is discussed openly with your child, outsiders should not be privy to the information. You have no way of knowing what a child can hear on the outside. If children are completely in the dark about their parents' divorce, the impact on them will be far more serious if they find out by accident. They cannot even begin to ask questions or voice their fear and anxiety to anyone. They may actually think that it is a secret and be afraid of what will happen to them if their parents find out that they know. By the time the parents do tell them the children may have created all kinds of fantasies and imagined problems that must now also be dealt with. Remember not to mention your impending divorce to outsiders until you have told it to and thoroughly discussed it with your children.

If children are properly prepared for the divorce, it can help them cope with what is to come without the loss of confidence and trust in their parents. Children need to know that even during the time of a divorce their parents are still capable of making decisions in structuring their own lives as well as those of their children. You do not want your child to lose confidence in you as a parent. The way you initially tell him or her about your divorce will have a lot to do with the child's continuing trust and respect.

Only the child's parents are in a position to allay the child's fears and accurately to tell him or her what to expect. This free-flowing communication between parent and child is basic to the emotional climate necessary for the child to learn to accept the divorce. The child's reaction can be very seriously undermined when he or she accidentally finds out what is happening.

Children should not be told about a divorce too far ahead of the actual separation. If you tell them weeks in advance that one of you is moving out and no move occurs, either you aggravate an unpleasant period or the children raise false hopes, further complicating a difficult and unpleasant situation. Conversely, telling children on the evening one parent is to leave the home is so shocking that it can cause severe emotional consequences.

Once you have established a definite day for moving out, it should not be changed. Doing so will again create false hopes that there will really be no departure. Remember, your children are extremely vulnerable at this time and your indecision will only further confuse and upset them.

There is no set formula for parents to use in introducing the subject of divorce to the children. This is not a once and for all pronouncement that begins and ends the subject with a single conversation. Children will need time to understand what the divorce is all about, gradually, according to their own ability to comprehend. They will not really begin to understand until they have lived the new life-style which the divorce will create.

Your child will not be able to grasp everything all at one time. Do not attempt to overload him or her the first time the subject is discussed. There will be plenty of other opportunities to elaborate on details.

Every parent will have his or her unique words to use. There is no such thing as just the right word or phrase. Meanings are conveyed by more than just words. Children will associate the meaning of the divorce with the verbal explanations a parent uses and also the attitudes and feelings conveyed by their parents' inflections, expressions, and appearances. Children are very sensitive to parental attitudes and feelings. Parents who are ashamed and reticent about their divorce are telling their children that what they are about to do is something shameful. Many children who have not even learned what society is all about develop a feeling of unacceptability about themselves because their parents are divorced. Very often these children have unconsciously internalized the feelings they see reflected in their parents' attitudes.

Parents who are positive and accepting about their divorce show their children that they have done nothing wrong and are very much the same people they were before. And parents who are anxious over their divorce and terribly distraught will probably project these feelings onto their children. This will only compound the anxiety the children already have.

Parents should be very aware of their own feelings about their divorce before they tell their children about it. First impressions last a long time. Children will remember the feeling and mood longer than the words they heard.

Parents should settle the major issues privately. You must decide where and with whom the children will live and where the absent parent will live. You must also make arrangements for visitation before breaking the news to your children.

Do not treat such a conversation as though it were routine table talk. Allow plenty of time for it. It is vital that both parents try to be present. Remember you are telling your children that one of the people they are most dependent upon is about to leave the household. Because, in essence, this is what a divorce means to them.

In *What About Me?* and *The Family That Changed,* I discuss a child's fear of losing a parent. Children need constant reassurance that they are as important to you as ever, that neither of you will stop loving them. That, because you are unhappy with each other, in no way means you are unhappy with your children. Regardless of how they react initially, children must be reassured that they are not losing a parent. Be patient with them. Children need time to accept and digest the divorce and all its attendant ramifications.

Although you must be prepared to answer all the children's questions honestly, do not be too eager to offer more information than they are ready for. *Take your cues from them.* They cannot be expected to grasp everything at once. There is little point in trying to give a distraught child all the details in one sitting. There will be plenty of other opportunities to elaborate. Many children will be most anxious to know where they will live and with whom, and how often they will be able to visit the parent with whom they do not live. Be prepared to give them definite answers, should they ask.

Your children's understanding of your divorce will develop for many years to come. Growing children look to their parents as their primary source of knowledge. The divorce will not change this. As your life and your child's life continue to develop and change, so will your child's ideas about how the divorce has influenced things. Your child will probably be closely watching the things you do in an attempt to understand why your divorce happened at all. He or she may look at things more critically and with more skepticism than before. Parents who explain the divorce thoroughly and keep their children properly informed about the progress of the divorce are helping the children solidify their confidence in their parents. Children want to believe in their parents and will go to every extreme in an attempt to do so. Even in the most adverse conditions, children will often color things to suit themselves in an attempt to maintain a strong parental image. Children need to rely on their parents and to trust them. The way you allow your children to question you about your divorce and the way you answer will determine whether you will keep their confidence. They must know that they are free to inquire and you will help them to understand what they need to know.

At pivotal ages in your children's development they will see things differently. But this is what growth is all about. Once your divorce is an established part of your children's lives, it will become a permanent addition to their total life experience, subject to reinterpretation during different stages in their development. Your child's questions and understanding should not be limited to the early days, or even years, following your divorce. Your willingness to help him or her should continue for as long as questions arise.

I have known parents who have told me how their daughter or son wanted to know all the details of their parents' divorce some fifteen years later, when they were on the brink of their own marriage. The child had spent endless hours trying to understand how and why his parents' marriage failed. The child's freedom to inquire is a very important part of a strong parent-child relationship.

In any type of interpersonal communication between people, be it parent-child, husband-wife, child-to-child, or adult-to-adult, there is always present an element beyond the spoken words. As I have previously stated, the emotional tone can often be more meaningful than the words themselves. This applies not only to breaking the news about the divorce but to all discussions thereafter.

Yet this does not mean that what you *say* is not important. The unpleasantness of what you have to say can still be minimized rather than exaggerated. Careful planning and a lot of thought on the part of both parents will prepare you to attempt to explain things to your children. I use the word "attempt" because, particularly when it comes to children, you can never be 100 percent sure about anything. But in spite of this it is still wise for parents to preplan and have clear ideas about what they will say to their children before they are actually engaged in the conversation.

One approach is to try to explain to them how different things happen to all of us every day. Some we like and some we don't like. Some of the things that we don't like, we can sometimes change. Explain that you are no longer happy being married to your husband or wife. This is one of the things that you can change. You do not have to continue being married to someone you are unhappy living with. Continue to explain to your child that if you had stayed married to each other you would have continued making each other very unhappy. But instead you made a decision to change all this. You are getting, or have gotten, divorced because you no longer are happy living together. If this is an honest expression of your feelings, and you say it with a great deal of tenderness, it will help to soften the words for your child. Children must learn to accept their parents' right to feel in the same way as they demand the right to have their own feelings. It is difficult for children to conceive of their parents' happiness being anything that is so radically different from their own. Children are very egocentric in the way they see the world. Parents exist for their children's convenience. You must try gently to demonstrate that, in addition to being a parent, one is still a person who has the right to find his or her own happiness.

If your child is old enough to understand the legality of marriage and divorce, try to explain it. Explain that by law you could not stay married to each other and still find happiness with someone else. But if you are divorced, you would each have a chance to find someone else to marry and with whom to share your life. Some parents prefer not to mention the idea of another marriage at this time. Unless this possibility is imminent, it is not essential to concern a child with this now. There is plenty of time to introduce the notion of remarriage after a child has come to terms with the more basic acceptance of the divorce. In chapters 10 and 11 on remarriage in *What About Me?*, I discuss what some parents unwittingly do that often leads to serious problems at the time of remarriage. Please be sure to read that section.

Of course when children seem to be overly concerned about the prospects of your remarrying and ask very direct questions, you must answer them. Children can be quite fearful over what will happen to them if you marry someone else. Most of their questions are all looking for one thing: the reassurance that they will not be forgotten and excluded from your life with someone else. They must be assured that they are a part of you now and will always remain a very important part of you whatever the future brings. The chapters on remarriage in this book and in *What About Me?* will give parents many insights into how to handle this topic with children.

The age of children will have a great deal to do with how and when they should be told. When there are both younger and older children involved you might decide to tell them separately, since they will not be able to comprehend at the same level. You should not attempt to explain to a five-year-old child in the same way that you would to a twelve-year-old.

There may also be instances where even though children are close to each other in age, parents may feel that it is better to talk to each of them separately. As a rule, however, children who are close in age and at similar intellectual levels can be very supportive of each other and find comfort in each other's presence at a time such as this. Therefore it is a good idea to talk to all the concerned children at the same time when the circumstances permit.

Each child is an individual and the parent's knowledge of a child should dictate whether to tell him or her alone or with other siblings present. But regardless of the age of the children or whether you tell them together or separately, both parents should be present at the time of the initial conversation. The presence of both parents can ease the impact of what is being said. Remember, your children are now being told that the two people they are most dependent on and emotionally tied to, with whom they have so far spent their entire lives, are about to do something that will remove one of them from the child's daily life. In essence, this is initially what divorce means to children, especially when they are still at an age when they consider everything in their environment only as it affects them.

Part of being a child is believing oneself the center of the universe. Children go through very painful experiences during the process of growing up, learning that the world does not exist solely for their enjoyment. Your divorce may be the first harsh awakening to the realities of life for a child at this stage.

The cardinal rule for parents to remember at all times, especially when they first tell their children about their divorce, is, be honest. The worst mistake many parents make is trying to conceal the true meaning of a divorce. They try to hide the truth by saying that one spouse is going on a trip or some other such fabrication. This kind of deceitfulness only confuses a child more and in the end makes it harder for the child to know what is really true. I cannot emphasize enough how important it is for a child to enjoy the trust of his or her parents and be able to rely upon truthful answers.

Growing children look to their parents as their primary source of guidance, support, and love. For parents to tell their children that "nothing is going to change" is as unrealistic as expecting them to believe it. Be honest. Children are bound to be anxious about how the change is going to affect them. Their questions will reflect this uncertainty. Both parents should agree on what they will tell their children and remain consistent no matter how often they are asked the same questions. This repetitive questioning can be a child's way of testing their parents to see if the answers remain the same. Your consistency is reassuring.

Perhaps the most difficult time for children to be involved in a divorce is during the adolescent years, particularly between the ages of ten to fifteen. Special consideration should be given to telling the adolescent child about the divorce.

This is a tremendously turbulent, emotionally disruptive time in the development of a child's personality and his adjustment to the adult world even when divorce is not present. Children at this time are going through major identity crises, trying to come to terms with who they are and what kind of persons they are going to be. They are extremely aware of peer pressure and terribly anxious to conform to their accepted peer group.

Anything that makes them different is to be avoided. When their parents suddenly present them with the trauma of a divorce, they can be overwhelmed with how this can set them apart from everyone else.

Parents who are familiar with what goes on during adolescence are better able to guide their children during the adjustment to the divorce.

It is not the purpose of this book to offer in-depth analysis of adolescence, or of any other stage of childhood. A reference list of excellent books on child development will be found in the Appendix. If you have not already done so, it would be well to read those books that pertain to your child's age group.

Adolescence at best usually creates a great deal of friction between parents and children. When divorce occurs, it is not unusual for children to attribute all their present difficulties to the divorce. They do not realize that many of their feelings would have been present anyway at this time in their development. Their belief that the divorce is to blame only compounds the problems that are in fact a result of the divorce, and makes the problems that are not that much more difficult for everyone to contend with. It is often difficult for all involved to know how to separate the two.

The child of thirteen or fourteen can sometimes appear to be very mature physically, mentally, or both. This is often very deceiving to parents. It leads them to believe that this child can handle the emotional trauma of divorce with much greater stability than a younger child. This is often quite untrue. The older child can have a far more difficult time accepting the divorce and often regresses to the emotional level of nine or ten or younger. He or she is not really capable of reacting emotionally at the level of maturity one expects of his or her age. Parents should keep this in mind and not become frustrated by what appears to be an older child's lack of cooperation or difficulty in accepting the divorce.

Sometimes parents are surprised when their younger children show less emotional disturbance than do the older ones. Often younger children do not grasp fully the meaning of the divorce. It is only after the passage of time, giving them a chance to live under the new conditions, that they begin to understand the significance of what has happened. Younger children may have a delayed reaction to the effects of the divorce and not really show any signs of emotional problems until much later.

For example, parents are often delighted when their five-year-old son or daughter reacts to being told about the divorce by saying, "Okay, can I watch television now?" These parents may think that the child is not upset and that they have done an admirable job of explaining the divorce to him or her. In reality the child has understood little and will only begin to react after experiencing the new conditions.

3

Accepting the Reality of Divorce:
Children's Feelings

Love

After a divorce many adults, overwhelmed by their own feelings, are not able fully to consider the emotional needs of their children. Chapters 2, 3, and 4 about feelings in *What About Me?* are designed to help your child understand his or her own feelings. In this chapter I point out some problematical areas that parents should be particularly aware of.

The concept of love, often a confusing emotion for adults, can be especially confusing for children at this time. Children may wonder why their parents have stopped loving each other. This is often a difficult question for an adult to answer for him- or herself, let alone his or her child. What a child may really want to know is what caused his mother and father to fall out of love. Considering the fact that a child does not yet understand what falling *in* love is all about, trying to explain how one falls *out* of love is even more difficult.

Parents should not invent reasons for what caused them to fall out of love. Nor should they compound the difficulties by heaping all the blame on their ex-spouses or on outsiders (the "other" man or woman or in-laws). Make sure your explanations do not create any new conflicts for your children. A safe approach is to assure your children that although you no longer love their father or mother, it has nothing to do with your feelings for them. They are not responsible for your feelings. Explain that you cannot pick a day or a time when you stop loving someone. It does not happen all at once. It happens a little bit at a time. When you begin to love someone, your feelings grow very slowly, and when you stop, they begin to diminish very slowly.

After a divorce children often worry that their parents will stop loving them because they have stopped loving each other. Parents must re-assure children constantly that this is not what happens.

In *What About Me?*, children learn that there are many kinds of love. The love between two adults is different from the love of a parent for a child. While a man and a woman can stop loving each other, a parent does not stop loving a child. Parents want to protect and take care of their children, and this love continues all through a child's life.

Young children often think that when parents are divorced the absent parent ceases to be their mother or father. Explain to them that although you are no longer married to each other you will *always* be their mother and father. A divorce cannot change that.

Let your children know that they are lovable and make them feel worthy of being loved. Do not assume your children know that you love them. They are looking for and need the comfort and reassurance that you can give them. There is a great deal to be gained from hearing a parent say "I love you, simply because you are my child and very special to me. Nothing between your father (or mother) and me can change the way I feel about you. You are a part of me and I will always love you." This may seem simple to an adult but children often need to hear a parent reaffirm his or her continued commitment to them. It is important to tell your child that you love him or her.

At a time of emotional upheaval children should be given guidance and help in dealing with their feelings. They often feel ambivalent toward their parents. To feel anger and resentment toward people one loves can be confusing and painful. The love that they are supposed to feel has turned to what they think is hate or anger. These can be very frightening feelings for children to have to live with, especially if they are afraid that someone will find out that they feel this way. These feelings can cause a great deal of present unhappiness and many future problems. Children do not realize that even though you love someone, your feelings can change and that you can be angry at and even think you hate the very parent you love and depend on so much. It is up to an aware parent to help his or her child realize that these feelings are temporary, normal, and to be expected, without feeling guilty about them. Children must be told that they are not bad for feeling this way. They must be shown by love and understanding that you, their parent, can love them and care for them even if they are feeling ambivalent toward you. Let them know that you understand how they feel. Do not blame them for feeling angry. They have a right to be angry and hurt over something which they had nothing to do with. It always helps children to know that their parents understand and care how they feel and that they are not considered "bad" by parents because of their feelings. You should try to help them learn to voice their feelings and express them openly. Only then will they be able to come to terms with all the hostility they feel inside.

Anger

Just as complicated as helping children come to terms with their ambivalent feelings of love is helping them understand their anger and what it can do to them. Anger is one of the most difficult feelings for them to contend with at this time. Many children are so motivated by anger now that it dominates every aspect of their behavior, to the detriment of all concerned. They should be helped to understand that just as there are different kinds of love there are different kinds of anger. In order for children to learn to contend with their anger, they must be helped to understand that your divorce is something they cannot change no matter what they think about it. It can be difficult for children to tell the difference between what they can change and what they cannot. Their refusal to accept the finality of your divorce is often related to their believing they can change what has happened. There is a difference between anger that leads to constructive action and anger that is destructive and inhibits one's feelings. You can help your child understand this difference by making up stories that contain examples of how anger works. Or use the examples provided in *What About Me?*

Point out that some of the things that make us angry, we are unable to change no matter how angry we get. Eventually what you must try to make them understand is that your divorce is one of the things they cannot change and that no matter how angry they are it will not change the divorce. Children often think that just because they do not like something they can change it. We as adults know this is not so. But you should not take it for granted that your child also realizes this. Much of the anger and hostility your child feels is often directed toward trying to change what has happened. When this does not work, it only creates stronger feelings of anger and hostility. A child needs the intervention and guidance of a knowing adult to help curtail the destructive anger he or she is feeling. Often sitting down and talking to children, telling them that "no matter how angry you are about what has happened, your anger cannot change anything" can help. Explain that all that being angry can do is

[16]

make them very sad and unhappy. Let them know that you understand their anger and do not blame them for feeling that way. This will not get rid of their feelings but sometimes it helps the children just to know that their parents know and care about how they feel. It spares a child the agony of being alone and isolated from the parents he or she really loves.

Denial

Parents do not always realize that their children are finding difficulty in accepting the divorce. For example, eight-year-old Peter's ready smile and placid demeanor seemed to indicate that he was adjusting well. But every day after school he took half his lunch money and threw it into the wishing well in the park and wished his parents were not divorced. A child's difficulty in accepting the divorce may be transformed into a pretense that it has not really happened.

Mary, eleven, said a special prayer each night for God to bring her parents back together. Children often think they have the power to make what they wish or believe come true.

Let your children know that you are telling their teachers about your divorce. It is important that personnel at school be made aware of the change in your marital status in order to be alert to any unusual behavior on the part of the child. Most teachers are anxious to cooperate in these situations. When your child sees you have nothing to hide it will help him or her accept that divorce is not a secret or anything to be ashamed of. Your account of the divorce to the teacher is also a definite sign that establishes the validity and finality of the divorce.

Encourage your child to bring friends home, especially at dinner time or perhaps for a sleep-over. Children who are having a denial problem will usually hesitate and not want to bring friends home for fear that they will find out about the divorce. They don't want to have to answer any questions about where their father may be, or why they are living with their father now and not their mother. The fear of exposure is so threatening to them that they can no longer enjoy inviting friends to their home. In order for you to deal with this problem, you must be aware that it is happening.

One of the best ways of finding out how your child is handling things is to ask the child. There is nothing wrong with asking a child what he has told his friends concerning your divorce. Ask how he feels when talking about it with his friends. Be extremely positive in the attitude you use when you discuss this. Do not make it appear that you anticipate he is having problems. You are not prying or being nosy. You are a concerned parent. Children appreciate knowing that their parents care about how they feel. Let your children know that you are concerned about their feelings and you understand that they may be having problems explaining things to their friends.

Some children might even welcome suggestions from their parent on what to tell their friends when they ask questions. What they tell their friends will be determined somewhat by what you tell them. It is very important to assure children that they will always have their mother and father and that their two parents will always love them and be concerned about what happens to them. In fact, you should *insist* that they will always have their mother and father; that they are not losing either of you. *What About Me?* and *The Family That Changed* contain discussions of many of the fears and apprehensions children will have. These fears can be eased tremendously by your awareness that they exist and your understanding and reassurance. By reading the appropriate children's book yourself, you will be better prepared to anticipate and cope with your child's apprehensions.

Since much of what a parent will tell a child will influence what the child tells his or her friends, it is important that a child be confident in what he or she has been told. Truthfulness and honesty are essential. Only then will children have the courage to tell friends that their parents are simply not living together anymore, but that they both still love them and that they will always have a mother and father the same as before the divorce.

If you discover that your child is having a denial problem, you must do something to help him or her to resolve it. Most children who are having this problem do so because they are ashamed of their parents' divorce and feel tremendous peer pressure over being different. They think that they have done something wrong and begin to feel doubts about themselves and their parents. This is especially true of the adolescent child but it can happen to younger children as well. Peer identity is a very important thing to a child at any age. Most children try to be like their friends. They usually try to dress alike, comb their hair the same way, and even speak with the same expressions. Any parent who has tried to convince a boy to get a crew cut when all his friends have full heads of hair, or a girl to wear a pretty party dress to a dance when all her friends will be in jeans, knows how difficult this is. Children need to know they belong to more than just their family. Friends are a very important part of the world in which they are trying to find a place. When something happens that makes them different from their friends, they do not like it. When all their friends' parents are married and their parents are divorced it can make them feel they are not as good as their friends and that they must now hide the shame of what has happened to their family. It is not easy for an adult to persuade a child who feels this way that it is foolish and unwarranted. A child may find it very difficult to control the feeling of shame and guilt he or she is having. Bear in mind that no child is feeling this way out of choice.

The adolescent child even more than children of other ages needs to feel that his or her parents' divorce does not reflect on his or her basic worth. Adolescence is a time when children will reexamine family relationships in search of their own growing identities. Therefore, it is important that they feel secure about their own place in a family, especially in a family that is about to experience the divorce of the parents.

Helping children come to terms with feelings of anger and denial cannot be accomplished overnight, nor is it an easy job. It takes patience and guidance on the part of both father and mother. Hoping your child will outgrow his or her present feelings of anxiety is not realistic. If you do not feel that you can handle this on your own, you might want to talk to someone who can give you direction and insight. There are many organizations today that offer just this kind of service on a private basis, or in a group. It is often not as expensive as parents anticipate to get a few sessions of guidance counseling for themselves or their child. Sometimes this is all that is needed to begin to turn the corner. The mental health service in your local community can probably advise you where such services can be found.

Do not make the error of simply trusting to chance and assuming that everything will eventually work itself out. Cries for help are often disguised. Few children are able to come right out and ask for help.

Guilt can really plague a child during the time of his or her parents' divorce. We as adults know how burdensome it is to carry around the pressure of guilt for something we have done. A sense of responsibility that is created by guilt has been known to produce all kinds of neuroses in adults.

Guilt

Guilt can be an extremely troublesome feeling for children because it often hides behind other feelings. It is sometimes difficult for children to know they are feeling guilty. Yet the guilt they are feeling becomes an unconscious motivator for their outward behavior. It is important to help a child recognize what guilt is so he or she can identify it as a feeling he or she may be having. It is not easy to explain things as abstract as anger and guilt to a child. Nevertheless it must be done. You can begin by talking about these feelings with your child and giving him or her examples of how these feelings actually can make one behave. If a person blames him- or herself and keeps feeling responsible for something that has happened, that person is feeling guilty. Many children blame themselves for their parents' divorce and harbor all kinds of guilt feelings about how and why they did this.

The children's book *What About Me?* contains examples of guilt. They are something a child can relate to and identify with. Once you have established an understanding of what guilt is all about, you can then attempt to relate these feelings to your divorce and show your child how he or she may feel as a result of harboring guilt feelings about being the cause of your divorce. Helping your child bring these feelings, if they exist, into the open is the best way of coping with them. They may not disappear overnight but they will certainly begin to diminish.

Once you have gone this far you are better able to help your child understand how his or her anger and guilt are making him or her behave. Some children feel so guilty about the angry feelings they have toward their parents that it makes them feel sad all the time.

Most of the time children can understand what it is that is making them feel angry and they can do something to make their angry feelings go away. But when angry feelings become mixed with disappointment and guilt, they can be very difficult to control. This is when your child needs your help to overcome his confusion and misery.

No matter how terrible the things your child is feeling or saying are, you must assure him or her that you will not stop loving him or her. The sooner you can encourage children to start talking about all these feelings bottled up inside, the better they will begin to feel and the faster the guilt and anger will go away.

Wishing

Children often confuse wishing with reality and think that just because they wished something to happen it did happen.

Susan wanted a part in the school play but the teacher picked someone else. Sue was disappointed and angry at her teacher. She wished something terrible would happen to her. The next day someone spilled paint on the floor and the teacher slipped and fell and was taken to the hospital. Susan was frightened. What if people knew what she had been thinking? Would they blame her for the accident? She thought she might never be allowed to go to school again.

Children who have had angry thoughts about their parents in the past may now feel that the divorce was their doing. They must be helped to understand that a mother does not go away from home because her daughter wished she would, or that a father left because his son was jealous of him. Tell them that their wishes cannot make something happen; that wishing something awful would happen to you did not cause your divorce.

Parents often wonder what caused children to feel this way. It seems so absurd to think that they would blame themselves for the divorce and actually have guilt feelings about it.

One of the real joys of childhood is innocence and the magic world of make-believe into which children's imaginations can carry them. Imagination is the key to so much of the fantasy world in which children live. Imagination has a great deal to do with the hypothetical demons that haunt a child during the time of a divorce.

Parents must try very hard to discover what is really behind a child's anger and belligerence when it is excessive. Children are not unhappy and disobedient merely because they want to be a source of annoyance and get attention. A sad, unhappy child, full of rebellion and anger, needs help.

Younger children may have a delayed reaction to the effects of the divorce and not show any signs of distress until much later. Many parents have taken a great deal of time to explain everything very clearly and are sure their child understands what he or she had been told, only to have the child ask later, "What is a divorce? Who are you talking about that is getting one?" Words are not always the best way to communicate an abstract idea to young children. In addition to being told, they need time to live with it.

Coming to terms with one's feelings is no easy job, whether you are a child or an adult. Considering all the difficulty adults have in this area it is not surprising that children can have even more problems.

4

Separation vs. the Divorce

It is not unusual today to meet parents who tell you they are not divorced, they are only separated. Although there is a definite legal difference between being divorced and separated, the emotional impact of the two is often very much the same. A child is not interested in the legality of whether his or her parents are divorced or separated. To children, all that really matters is that their parents are no longer living together and that their own lives have changed since one of their parents moved away.

Parents sometimes make the mistake of thinking that because they are only separated on a trial basis, they do not really have to explain anything to their children. After all, it is only a trial arrangement and they may come together again. Although this may be so and their intentions may be honestly to see how it will feel living without each other, it is not so simple for the children.

Telling a child that you are trying separation is not much different from telling a child you are getting a divorce. To the child, the result of what is happening is the same. His or her mother and father are no longer living together as a family. And that is what is important to them.

Depending on the age of the children involved, trial separations are very unfair to children because they do not draw clear boundaries for what the child can expect. Children are left in a constant state of hoping and wishing that their parents will get back together. Trial separations also leave parents in a constant state of making up their minds. Yet many adults feel that a trial separation is the only way that they can tell if they are really suited for each other or better off apart. Sometimes a husband and wife may decide that one of them will go away on an extended trip in an attempt to come to terms with feelings. Anything that removes you from the reality of your daily life, however, is certainly not a good way to determine the future of your marriage. Yet adults may decide that this is one way of sorting things out. They may simply tell their children that the absent parent had to go away on an extended trip and will return soon. Both parents then continue to cover up the real reason for the absence in hopes of sparing the children any undue concern prematurely. The couple's hope is that, other than missing the absent parent, the children will not be aware that there is a problem.

I believe that such an arrangement is unfair to both the adults and children involved. A separation that does not involve the responsibilities of one's daily life cannot realistically reflect the position of your marriage. Assuming that you decide to get a divorce at the end of this vacation, what do you now tell your children? Remember, you have told them all along that the missing parent is only away on business or a vacation. It will not take much for a child to realize that this was only a half-truth. When that happens it is much more difficult to retain the child's trust and respect. Knowing that he or she can still trust both parents is very important in helping the child accept the divorce.

During a trial separation, nothing of a permanent nature can be resolved and the children are left in a quandary. What they can be told is that their parents are not happy living together and want to try living apart. Parents who are undecided about wanting to remain with each other inflict a tremendous burden upon their children. Even very young children somehow sense the mixed feelings their parents have and try to become matchmakers to bring their parents together again. Imagine the children's disappointment if all their efforts fail. They may even begin to believe that they are partly responsible for their parents' divorce.

To a child, a trial separation is very much like saying that someone is both dead and alive at the same time. That certainly sounds confusing. But that is precisely what a trial separation does to a child. You are saying that you can not live either with or without each other. This indecisiveness shows your children that you are not sure of your feelings regarding their father or mother. You may even be creating fear in your children about whether you have the same uncertain feelings about *them*. Since your trial separation is just that, you are not in a position to give any definite answers to your children's questions.

For all the drawbacks, there are times that a trial separation can save a marriage and make people realize how much they belong together. I certainly would not negate the value of anything that can save a marriage. But parents should be aware of the turmoil they are creating in their children's lives.

If a trial separation is the only suitable answer to your marital problems, it should be explained to the children in much the same way as a divorce. That is, appropriate to children's ages, the temporary nature of what you are doing and the uncertainty you both feel toward each other need not be stressed. Children should be made aware of the fact that one of their parents is moving out. The why should be an honest explanation to the children that their parents are not happy living together and are going to try to live apart from each other for a while. You must be prepared to answer all the questions children may have about what will happen if you decide never to live together again. Although your children may not realize what they are asking, they really want to know what will happen if you get a divorce. As premature as this may sound to you, it is something you must be prepared to talk about if your children ask. You must be prepared for your children to ask on a daily basis when their mother or father is coming back home again.

As you can see, the precariousness of a trial separation leaves children in a very vulnerable position. Although I would never suggest that parents be anything but honest with their children, it is often not necessary to spell things out in such detail that a child is oversaturated with knowledge. It is more advisable to proceed as though you were expecting to divorce.

I would keep all efforts at reconciliation purely between the adults involved. It is unfair to involve your children in your attempts. Do not encourage their hopes in this direction or suggest to them that you will soon be back together again if that is not the case. Remember your children will be anxiously—almost daily—awaiting the reuniting of their parents. Even though they may eventually stop asking and appear to have settled into your temporary way of life, they are still full of hope. The faster you can determine the future of your marriage, the better off the children and you will be.

Just a word of clarification. Since all divorces must go through a legal period of separation before becoming final, I am not referring to this aspect of being separated. Under these circumstances, a separation is approached from the point of view of the pending divorce and it is possible to set definite boundaries on what will be taking place. Children can be told what to expect and decisions can be made regarding everyone's future. The family can actually begin living as though the divorce were final, with few exceptions.

5

What Do I Tell My Friends and Relatives?

As mentioned earlier, divorce is no longer scandalous or shocking. Most of us know someone who has been divorced. Yet, it is still an event that may arouse curiosity and speculation among one's friends, neighbors, and relatives.

Some individuals are very private people who prefer to keep everything to themselves. In times of stress, however, many of us cannot resist seeking comfort and sympathy from any friends who are willing to listen.

Children can easily be victimized by the things a parent says to friends in moments of anger: Your friends or relatives will talk among themselves and may repeat—and embellish—what you tell them. *Their* children may also overhear these conversations. No parent wants children to come home from school crying because they were asked if their father really has a girl friend, or if their mother drinks.

One cannot stop people from gossiping but one does not have to provide the material on which it is based.

Suzanne B. had a safe way of venting the anger she felt toward her ex-husband. She would tell it all to her tape recorder, privately, and then play it back. After listening to some of the harsh, bitter things she said, she was glad no one else had heard them. Fortunately, she could erase the tapes.

It may help to write down all your recriminations. By the time you finish reading them, you will probably want to tear up the notes. Or you can say it all to yourself out loud and be glad there is no one around to hear you. The important thing is not to expose deep private feelings to outsiders.

If a husband and wife can agree to limit what they tell others about their divorce, *everyone* will be much better off.

What a child will say to friends can also present a problem. Most children want to be like their friends. We have discussed this identity need in previous chapters. Children plagued by feelings of shame and guilt will have problems with their friends.

Ellen is a good example of this. When her sixth grade class put on a school play, the parents were invited. Ellen asked her mother and father to sit together so the other children would not know they were divorced. Although Ellen's parents had openly discussed their divorce with their friends, they had assumed mistakenly that she had done the same with her friends.

"Why didn't you tell your friends?" her mother asked.

"Because I don't want to be different."

"Why should our divorce make you different?"

"I don't know! I thought maybe my friends wouldn't like me anymore or they might think you're not good parents."

"Oh! Don't you think you have good parents?" Ellen's mother asked.

Ellen hesitated. "Well, no!" she burst out. "Because if you were *really* good parents, who cared about me, you would never have gotten divorced. All my friends have fathers who come home at night, except me."

Her mother had had no idea that Ellen felt this way. Ellen felt her parents had betrayed her. She thought that if other people knew about the divorce they would feel the same way about her parents that she did. Worst of all, Ellen felt her parents' divorce had made her different.

It is useless for an adult to tell a child that his or her feelings are unwarranted. Her mother did not reprimand Ellen or scold her for expressing her feelings. She explained that the divorce had not made Ellen different. Ellen had not changed. Her name was the same, her hair still curly, and her eyes still brown. Friends, Ellen's mother told her daughter, may be curious about our divorce because they do not always understand. But as time goes on everyone will learn that nothing terrible or mysterious has happened.

Children need to be reassured that their friends will not abandon them or feel differently about them. Encourage your child to bring friends home. We have already discussed how children handle activities with friends.

The kind of things you say and do with your own friends provides the best example, showing your child how to cope with curious friends' questions. Children often overhear (even when parents are not aware) the things you say to your friends and will probably latch on to much of this for their own conversations. Friends can be a very important outlet for children at this time. Parents must be sure to encourage their children to continue their friendships and not allow the divorce to interfere.

6

Grandparents

Grandparents are very special people at the time of a divorce. Their behavior will have a direct influence on both the children and the parents. Yet too often a grandparent does not know what to do or how to behave. Awkwardness and unfamiliarity with what is expected of them can often lead to unhappy situations.

Grandparents are often injured parties and usually do not have the luxury of anyone recognizing how involved they are. Parents are so preoccupied with the problems of their children and themselves that they do not observe the effect on the grandparents.

Many grandparents persist in trying to persuade the couple not to divorce. This often happens when there have been constant in-law problems. In-laws often blame themselves for creating the tension and friction that ultimately caused the breach. But they should know that a good marriage is rarely destroyed by in-laws nor is a bad one held together by them. Assuring your in-laws that they are not responsible for your decision to divorce is necessary at this time. They must be told by the divorcing couple that they are not to blame any more than the children are. Once you have made an irreversible decision, they should be told gently but firmly that they cannot persuade you differently. Explain that if they continue to pressure you, they only create more confusion for everyone. Suggest to them that you need their support and understanding for the sake of the children and yourself.

What is the real responsibility of grandparents in the event of the divorce of their child? The grandparent is both a parent to one of you and a grandparent to your children. All too often grandparents' views of their responsibility to their child is in conflict with what is in the best interest of their grandchildren.

Obviously grandparents are caught in the middle just as your children are but their problem is more complex. They must decide where to continue to give their support and allegiance. When a divorce leaves one spouse with bitterness and hurt it is only natural for the parents of this spouse to want to aid their child. Therefore, the son-in-law or daughter-in-law who was once loved now becomes the culprit, responsible for all misery everyone is suffering. The grandparents soon display the same bitterness and hurt as the divorcing couple, instead of being able to offer objective counsel, and be comforting and supportive. In-laws and grandparents frequently become bitter enemies. Obviously this only creates more tension and confusion for the children.

The last thing any divorcing couple needs is additional problems from in-laws. Although you are not directly responsible for how grandparents behave you can influence their behavior. Do not encourage your parents to place all the blame on your ex-spouse and ex-in-laws. When you make too much use of your parents as your sounding board, you encourage their constant interference. You cannot expect to expose all your anger and bitter feelings to them without creating the same feelings in them. They are only human and they will want to protect you at anyone's expense. Worst of all your children will recognize the dislike their grandparents now have for one of their parents.

I have heard many divorced couples complain that after many years their in-laws have remained bitter enemies even though the divorced couple themselves have now developed a friendly relationship.

Grandparents can be left with lasting scars after sharing their child's worst hours during the early days of the divorce. It is not always as easy for older people to forgive and forget. Just as the early days of your divorce will live with your children for years to come, so will these early days live with your parents.

If you take the time to explain to your parents what you expect of them, most will cooperate and want to respond in the most helpful way. Grandparents who continue to be meddlesome and unnecessarily controversial must be dealt with firmly but gently.

Explain to them that their interference is only hurting you more and certainly not helping your children. Point out how necessary their cooperation and understanding are at this time, especially to the children. Help them understand how helpful they can be to the children if they remain objective and neutral toward you and your ex-spouse. Their continued love and support for both you and your children can bring the greatest comfort to everyone.

Grandparents who force grandchildren to choose between their parents because they themselves have sided with one of the divorcing couple can do great damage. Point out to them that it is bad enough that the children are subjected to the separation of their parents. To see the animosity among their grandparents leaves the children no friendly direction in which to turn. Tell them that grandparents are not trained counselors and their attempts at arbitrating the couple's differences are usually not appreciated by anyone.

Point out that grandparents from both sides will still love their grandchildren and want to protect them and spare them all the pain they can. Grandparents who can remain friendly and refrain from speaking harshly about either of the parents provide genuine support for their grandchildren. They should tell their grandchildren, "No matter what happens between your parents we will always love you and want you." It confirms to their grandchildren that a kinship between the two families will still exist even after the divorce. Grandparents' stability can be very comforting to grandchildren, especially if their own parents are disturbed. Often grandparents are the only ones children can turn to in their darkest moments of need and confusion.

Even the most embittered grandparents will respond to this advice.

Grandparents are often taken for granted by the divorcing couple. For example, they may suddenly be expected to watch or care for the grandchildren when no one else seems to have time or be able to do so. Many grandparents have suddenly found themselves having to raise small children all over again. No grandparent should be expected to assume additional financial responsibilities because of your divorce.

In many instances the financial hardships of a divorce affect the grandparents. Most will want to help out and do all they can within their own budgets. It is unfair for grandchildren to constantly ask their grandparents for money because the chances are they will not be refused. Grandparents will often give up items they need to satisfy their children and grandchildren. But no one should take advantage of this. Obviously grandparents will be aware of the nature of your financial situation. Their knowledge of your circumstances should be all the pressure that is placed upon them for financial aid. Most grandparents will contribute all they can without being asked. If a grandparent has substantial wealth and refuses to help, there is nothing you can do. Even in such a situation it is wise to say nothing to the children and allow them to continue a warm relationship with their grandparents.

[31]

Grandparents are often placed in a quandary when their divorced child remarries and acquires additional children with the new marriage.

Most grandparents will be so happy to see that their child is part of a happy family unit once again that they will be very willing to embrace all members of the new family. They may even be a bit oversolicitous in the beginning in their attempt to show how accepting and approving they are. In this situation all you can do is let time enable everyone to find his best role.

Some grandparents, unable to accept new children in a remarriage, avoid any involvement with them. They may feel disloyal to their own grandchildren if they show friendship to your new stepchildren. Even though such feelings are unjustified, you cannot force your parents to display affection they do not feel. But you can tell them how fond you are of your new children and that you are now a total family. Explain how their total acceptance of your new family can make things much happier for everyone. They can contribute more to the success of your new life by joining in your new family and being receptive grandparents to everyone. Assure them that you do not expect them to respond immediately, but you would certainly like to feel that they are making every effort to accept your new children and husband or wife.

If you do not exclude them from your new life, acting as you probably did when you were married the first time, it may help. Even the most negative grandparents will begin to soften with repeated overtures of friendship and inclusion by you and your new family.

By all means explain to your new children (if they are old enough) that they are not responsible for the coolness or lack of affection your parents have toward them. Let them understand that your parents need time to accept your new family, and all you would like them to do for the time being is to be polite and friendly. Before long, you can explain, your parents will grow as fond of them as you are. Do not make the mistake of trying to tell children that someone loves them and wants them when they really do not. The children will sense this rejection by the adult and lose both confidence and trust in you for trying to deceive them. It is much better to be honest with the children and elicit their cooperation and understanding, especially if there is every chance that the situation will improve with time. The children themselves can do much to help reluctant grandparents feel more at ease. Do not be afraid to be honest with all your children. Even your own children can be helpful in telling their grandparents how happy it would make them if they became part of the family. How happy they would be for their grandparents to accept their new sister or brother. Assuring their grandparents that they are not resentful or jealous of sharing their attention and affection can reduce the grandparents' confusion.

If your parents seem to be having problems adjusting to your divorce, it may be necessary to suggest that they seek professional advice. Perhaps they might have a session with a marriage counselor or family service organization, a clergyman they are associated with, a family doctor, or a friend. But do suggest that they talk to someone. Confused people, regardless of age or status, need to talk about their problems. The sooner you can help them learn to accept your divorce and all its ramifications the easier things will be for you. Continuing to argue with them only creates harsh feelings and additional tension.

7

Deciding with Whom a Child Should Live

It is no longer taken for granted that after a divorce a child remains in the custody of the mother. Although this is often the practical and convenient solution it may not always be in the best interest of the child. This is not to suggest that parents become involved in a custody battle; rather they should be willing to analyze which parent can better meet the needs of the child.

Since a child has different needs at different stages of his or her life, the present role of each parent must be evaluated in order to decide who should retain custody.

Whether the children are old enough to have a reasonable preference for living with one parent or the other should be considered.

For toddlers and preschoolers the mother is usually the dominant figure. The more dependent a child is on someone else for his or her basic needs, the more critical that person's presence becomes to the child. This is not to suggest that a father is not important to or needed by a younger child as well. But younger children who spend much more time with a mother will often react to her absence with greater emotional distress.

In some families, however, the traditional roles of mother and father have been reversed. When the father has assumed the dominant role as caretaker, it may be preferable for him to retain custody.

The affective level of emotional exchange that exists between a parent and a child is not always synonymous with the fulfillment of immediate physical needs. Whatever the age of the child, the subtle intangible flow from a parent to his or her child will affect every aspect of the relationship. A danger lies in assuming that the parent the child appears to be more dependent on outwardly is really the parent with the closer ties. Very often the emotional nourishing and coddling a child needs to develop a positive self-image do not come from the parent who spends more time with the child. Although this parent may appear to be meeting the child's every need, he or she may only be doing so in a most custodial way. Such care can meet the outward needs of a child and not satisfy the emotional needs of a child.

In some families joint custody may be the solution. Some parents decide to set up separate homes close to each other, enabling the children to alternate between the two every few days. There is a great deal of controversy surrounding this type of living arrangement. Since there are no statistics or research to support or negate its value, no definitive conclusions can yet be drawn.

Although the identity children gain from both their parents is important at any age, the younger child is not as vulnerable to this need as the preadolescent and adolescent. An adolescent boy patterns much of his behavior after his father or father figure. Thus, it may be preferable for a teen-age boy to live with his father. Those who continue to live with their mothers should have frequent opportunities to spend time with their fathers.

Adolescent girls too have a particularly strong need for a father's presence. Because they are now beginning to form heterosexual relationships, it is important that girls be able to maintain their relationships with their fathers.

Children may want to know how their parents decided with whom they would live. The explanation should be direct and uncluttered by extraneous details. For example, one might say that since their mother and father are no longer going to be living together, and since the children are not old enough to live alone (nor would you want them to), it is necessary that they live with one parent at a time. It is your responsibility to see that they are properly cared for. Emphasize that while each of you wanted them very much, you had to decide on the one who was better able to care for them.

When parents are equally willing and able to retain custody, they may want to take the children's preference into consideration. But asking your child to choose which parent he or she would prefer to remain with is not recommended. It may make the decision easier for the parents but it is too great a responsibility to place upon a child. Most children who have very strong preferences will usually make this known. A grandparent, aunt, or uncle may be able to elicit a preference from a child without creating uncomfortable feelings in the child.

If you feel you need help in assessing the parent-child relationship, seek the opinion of a professional who will assist you in understanding how to evaluate your child's needs. The books on child development listed in the Bibliography will also be helpful.

8

Moving Out and Other Changes
(Relocating and Money Matters)

The day of a parent's departure can be traumatic for everyone. After all, this is what the divorce is all about. A child may plead and argue, or beg the parent not to go yet, to stay for just one more night. But one more night would become another and another. Anyone who has ever had to say good-bye to someone loved knows how hard that can be. Your children must be made to realize that they are not saying good-bye to you. They are merely letting you go through the door. You will be as much a part of them as you ever were. Your departure is not a permanent one; they will see you very soon.

Under no circumstances should a parent leave before the child has been fully prepared. The disappearance of a parent can destroy the child's faith and trust in both parents. Children should be told in advance what day a parent will be moving out. There should be no elaborate ceremony about this, no prolonged good-byes, no big send-off with everyone clustered around the door.

Packing should *not* start weeks in advance. Children should not have to stand around gaping while a parent packs suitcases and boxes. This should be done as inconspicuously as possible. Boxes and suitcases do not have to be left stacked in the living room for everyone to stare at and think about. There is no reason to take all your possessions with you when you leave. Things can be moved out gradually, in advance of your actual leaving, or after you have left. Let children retain some of their pleasant memories of their parents living together. Your going through the door should be almost as natural as always. But there should be a firm understanding that you will not return to live in the house. Of course, you will be coming back often to see them. If possible set a time and date for your next visit. If you move out in the morning, you might arrange to return for dinner and to say good night to the children, or to spend some time with them the next day. Some parents take their children with them to look over their new living quarters. Some parents decide to move out on a day when they can take their children with them and allow them to spend this first night in the departing parent's new living quarters.

After the departure, the remaining parent should have an activity planned to divert the child's attention. What you do should be decided by both parents, depending on what you think is best for your child.

If you have decided that the departing spouse is not to enter the house during visitation, it should be agreed upon beforehand. A parent should not attempt to violate this agreement by demanding to come in when the child is standing at the door. Conditions upon which parents agree should be respected by both. If a change is to be made, it should be discussed when the children are not around.

It is a shock for children to see their home in upheaval. If furniture is to be moved out, they should be told in advance, and not suddenly find a half empty home. It is also best that they not be present when the actual moving is done.

Witness the grandmother who arrived one afternoon with a moving van, and while the children sat on the steps, watching, removed all the living-room furniture she had given her son and daughter-in-law as a wedding gift. For weeks afterward, five-year-old Jerry woke up with nightmares because he thought the moving truck and his grandmother were coming to take *him* away. The child rarely went into the room after that, and was understandably uneasy in his grandmother's company.

Possessions are a very tangible part of a child's world. Parents may not be aware of the unconscious attachments children have to things in their homes. They derive great security from a familiar environment. During the time of a divorce, since so much is changing that cannot be avoided, it is advisable to let as much remain untouched in the home as possible.

When a divorce necessitates moving to a new home or area, a child is likely to experience increased difficulty in adjustment. There are several ways to minimize your children's anxiety.

Visit his or her school and arrange to meet the teacher before the child begins (preferably at the beginning of a new term). Ask the school for the names of classmates in your area and try to arrange to introduce your child to some of these children. Spend some time driving around or walking in the new neighborhood to familiarize the child with his or her surroundings. Visit the parks and library. Contact the local scout troop, youth club, or athletic club and visit it with your child.

When possible, reassure your child that he or she will still be able to see old friends. Tell him or her that you too will be making new friends.

You are also in the new situation and are just as anxious to readjust as he is or she is.

Money and Children

One of the things parents wonder about is whether or not to tell children about money matters. Especially if there are problems that did not exist before and money is tight.

The age of the child should decide what you do or do not discuss concerning money matters. Certainly a younger child who does not yet have any concept of what money is would only be confused by such conversations regardless of what you had to say.

But this is not the case with the adolescent child or teen-ager. In both these cases children are very aware of money and often concerned with their own spending power. Many children at these ages are given allowances and must learn to budget their own funds in order to have control of their lunch money and extra spending money. These children are very knowledgeable of what money can and cannot buy. They will probably be particularly aware of any major changes in their life-style that involve their ability to live as comfortably as before the divorce.

When a mother has had to go to work for financial reasons there is nothing wrong with explaining this to a child. After all, it is now necessary to run two separate houses or apartments, and many of the single expenses you had before are now doubled. An explanation such as this is a very logical and nonaccusatory way of explaining the situation. A child may be expected to cut back on some of his unnecessary spending habits as well. Perhaps he can bring lunch from home instead of buying it at school and maybe buy fewer magazines or other dispensable items.

It is never a good idea to burden a child with the weight of financial problems. But there is nothing wrong with telling a child that money may not be as free as it once was. Of course one parent should never blame this situation on the other. The actual financial arrangements that two parents have decided between them should remain between them. It is not necessary to reveal the details of these arrangements to the children. It is sufficient for them to know that their father is providing for them as well as he can and certainly trying to maintain their standard of living. The same should be said for a mother who is helping financially.

In many cases, in spite of both parents' financial efforts, it is not possible to maintain the standard of living the family enjoyed before the divorce.

If this is the case children should be told honestly that it will be necessary to curtail spending. Never should this situation be blamed on the inability of one or the other parent to provide the necessary funds.

In a case where a parent who has the funds to do so has refused to assume proper financial responsibility for the children, the children themselves will realize that they are not being treated fairly. Especially if they continue to see this parent living very comfortably. The children will readily distinguish the difference between their own circumstances and the affluence of the absent parent. But even in a case such as this it is not a good idea to criticize this parent before the children. The children have probably formed their own opinions about this parent's real interest in them. Your criticism does nothing to help the situation. If anything, refraining from expressing your own unhappiness about financial conditions will be much better for the children. Ultimately, when they have their own choice words to say about this parent, it would be wiser for you to avoid joining in.

When parents are honest with their children and share family matters with them it usually creates a very wholesome atmosphere. Children cooperate more willingly when they are taken into your confidence and understand what is going on. When children see that parents are trying to cooperate rather than blame each other for financial difficulties, it sets a pattern for them. It also encourages their desire to help in every way they can and reinforces the sense of love and trust they still want to have in their parents. Regardless of how difficult the financial situation may be, the tension is reduced when all family members are considerate and cooperative.

9

Visiting Days

Visiting days a child spends with the parent with whom he or she is not living can be either the most rewarding or most frustrating days of the month. Visiting days should be enjoyed by both parent and child. Unfortunately, this does not always happen.

If one parent has been used to having the other plan all the family outings when they were married, he or she may not know what to do with children on visiting days. Rigid plans, adhering to schedules, forced good fellowship, can ruin everyone's good time. This need not be the case. Visits should be as natural as possible. This is an opportunity for you to share time with your child to reinforce your relationship, to get to know each other. It is not always necessary to amuse him or her or provide unusual activities.

Visiting days were established by law to assure that both parents continue to see their children. Developing the parent-child relationship is the best way to use this time. Sharing warmth, companionship, and experiences can frequently be accomplished by simply walking in the park or riding a bicycle.

Of course, there will be times when you want to plan special outings. If the children are old enough, ask them for their suggestions. Some parents can get so carried away in planning activities they overlook consulting their children. Deciding together what special events you will go to makes children feel they are participants. If they are too young to contribute, you might ask your ex-spouse to help plan a day. This can be especially helpful for a father who is not used to spending a whole day with his young child. Friends with children of similar ages are also a good source of suggestions. In many cities there are books containing lists of local attractions. They can be obtained from libraries, bookstores, or chambers of commerce. Newspapers carry listings of events for children, many of which are free of charge. Having a good time and going places need not always cost much money.

Material things are never a substitute for real communication with your child. Continually buying toys to keep a child occupied contributes nothing toward building a relationship. Children need to be involved with parents on a level that relates to their needs. If a child is simply allowed to tag along on errands this will not enhance parent-child relationships. Taking your children along when you do your own shopping, or having them watch while you play tennis or while you work may result in their reluctance to see you on visiting days.

Mothers who visit with their children on a weekly basis usually have plenty to do when they see their children. The mistake many mothers make is that they do not devote enough of their time exclusively to their children. Being tuned into a child's needs, one would have to provide more than her presence. Children look forward to the visits they will have with their mother, especially if these visits are not too frequent, and they should be able to enjoy the togetherness. They are entitled to their mother's time and attention without the interference of other people.

In *What About Me?*, there is a special chapter on visiting days with a father and visiting days with a mother. In this chapter I point out some common problems that children have during their visits with their parent. Read this chapter carefully to determine whether, with the best intentions, you may be doing things that might be upsetting to your child.

There are times when parents overemphasize visiting days, permitting nothing, no matter how important, to interfere. A parent who makes children feel that without fail they must spend every weekend and school holiday with him or her may be forcing the children to miss a very important part of childhood. Some have such full school schedules that weekends are the only time they can spend with their peers. Going out with friends is important. Children may grow to feel guilty for preferring to be with friends instead of with their parent. Although a parent may feel he or she must see the child on each and every designated occasion, it is unfair to assume the child feels this way too. You will have a much happier relationship if your child has the freedom to tell you that he or she would rather go bowling or to the movies with friends than ice skating with you. There may also be times when you find you cannot spend a visiting day with your child. Your arrangements should be flexible enough to allow you to change these plans.

There is one cardinal rule that should be observed by all parents without any exception. Visitation rights should never be used as a manipulative tool to gain something you want or some advantage from an ex-spouse. The one who really loses when parents behave this way is the child. It is unfair to deprive your child of a visit or allow unpleasantness to mar the visit to which he or she looks forward.

Sometimes a parent may use the threat of withholding a visiting day as a punishment for something the child has done. This is a very poor means of discipline and should not be resorted to as a way of controlling a child's behavior. The visits a child shares with his or her parent should be treated as a special relationship set apart from all routine including discipline. There may be times when both parents agree to cancel a special activity that was planned for a visiting day because such a punishment relates to what the child has done. But the child should still be allowed to spend the day with the parent, minus the special event. When the time that a child has to spend with a parent is limited, it is unfair to interfere with these visits. It is more important that a child have the opportunity of developing the strongest possible relationship with the absent parent. There are many privileges other than visitation that can be withheld as a form of discipline.

Sometimes when a parent becomes obsessed with visiting days and feels that nothing can disrupt a visiting day, it can mean that the parent is compensating for guilt feelings still harbored about the divorce, or that he or she is feeling very insecure about the relationship with the child. Visiting days were not ordained. They were established as a legal way of assuring that both parents would continue to see their children.

Ideally, parental association with a child should be spontaneous and flexible, not something reduced to a designated day and time. Even if this is not in accord with your agreement, parents should come to an equitable arrangement regarding visitation that allows for spontaneity and flexibility. The divorce has given both parents the right to their own privacy. As such it is not realistic to expect to intrude on your ex-spouse without first giving advance notice. There may be times that your presence is not wanted and these feelings should be respected by both parents. But this does not mean that you cannot establish a working, equitable arrangement that allows for less rigidity in your visiting schedules. Definite plans can and should be made in advance. But you should also be able to telephone each other at nonspecified times to determine whether it would be convenient to see the children.

This type of arrangement will depend a great deal on how the parents can handle being in each other's company for any length of time. If they cannot tolerate each other's presence they will not want to encourage short and frequent visits. But this problem can be avoided if you do not remain together during these impromptu visits. By this I mean that the children can be taken someplace (to a park, for a walk, bicycle riding, for a soda, etc.) by the visiting parent, or the visiting parent can remain in the house while the other parent agrees to do chores away from the house, or perhaps visit a friend for an hour or so.

It is important that parents find a way to compromise on their differences so that the children will benefit.

Seeing as much of both parents as possible develops the healthiest relationships for a child. With this in mind, parents should try to work out as many possibilities as are practical for spontaneous visits. A decree from a court should not serve as the exclusive determinant on which visitations rest.

Children often try to use a father's visit or a mother's visit as a means of bringing the entire family together again. The children may still be wishing that a family picnic or some other activity will reunite the parents. There is nothing wrong with both parents occasionally doing something together, but if there is no chance for this to develop care must be taken not to give children false illusions or encourage their wish that their parents come together again.

Many parents feel very strongly about not doing things together. Some parents cannot tolerate being in the presence of their ex-spouses for any length of time. Other parents find that they are very uncomfortable in this kind of situation, whether contrived or not. And some parents simply do not want to give their children false hope.

Sharing activities with one's ex-spouse is a very personal matter. It should be decided by the adults on its own merit and not be prompted or manipulated by the children. If you are not comfortable going on outings with your ex-spouse and the children together, then by all means you should not do so. If children keep insisting on such an arrangement, there is nothing wrong with telling them that you prefer not to. As parents and adults you certainly can and should excercise whatever your judgment dictates is best in such a situation.

A word of caution: Often one parent wants the opportunity to get together with the ex-spouse, and tries to push just such a meeting through the children. He or she may even try to be included in the children's visit. This parent may actually turn the visit into an attempt to spend time with the ex-spouse. It is unfair to use the children as a front and interfere with their visiting day. Discuss such intentions with your ex-spouse privately, when the children are not present. Any such arrangements that you make should be concluded between the two of you.

It is desirable and indeed very preferable for children to see that their parents are amiable with each other and still have mutual respect for each other. But children do not belong in the private communications that you may want to have. Those only serve to confuse children and give them false hope.

Often when there is more than one child in the family a parent must remember that each of his or her children will want to have time alone with this parent. Visiting days are usually a collective venture, with everyone participating and present at the same time. Sometimes it is a good idea to discuss this with all the children, enlist their cooperation, so that each of them in turn will have a chance to be alone with each parent.

Parents should use discretion in deciding whether or not to bring a date or friend along with them on visiting days. A child should not have to compete for your interest and attention. It is not a good idea to expose your children to a steady flow of new people. On the other hand, a child may want to bring a friend along on visiting days. Do not discourage this. You may even suggest your child bring along a friend for a sleep-over at your home. Sleeping bags can be great fun for two or three children at a time. If children are relaxed enough to invite their friends, it is often a sign that they are adjusting well to the divorce.

I suggest that children read chapter 9 on visiting days in *What About Me?* with a parent (with each parent at a different time if necessary). This will give your child an excellent opportunity to point out anything that is disturbing him or her regarding your visiting day arrangements and activities.

10

Communicating with Your Child

Martin P's first visitation weekend with his daughter was an eye-opening experience. He found himself sitting across from her in a restaurant, fumbling for something to say, as if she were a stranger. He was confronted by the recognition that, while married, he had taken his relationship with his child for granted. Within weeks after this experience, Martin, like many parents without custody, began to complain of feeling shut out of his child's life.

Often, parents such as Martin feel that the money they provide is their only requirement for their children's upbringing. They resent the fact that the remaining parent is asserting influence and control over and enjoying the pleasure of intimacy with the child.

Divorced parents should be able to participate equally in rearing their children. Living apart from children does not mean playing a minor role in their lives. But it is necessary to think about and plan the kind of interaction that enables understanding to grow. Shared experiences form a natural basis for communication between a parent and child. All parents must establish situations that foster such opportunities, but it is especially important for divorced parents.

Roger L. saw Kevin only on alternate weekends. In order to maintain contact with him, he would telephone Kevin daily.

"Hi, Kevin, how are you today?"

"Okay, Dad, how are you?"

"Fine, son. How was school?"

"Great. I hit a double at recess and brought in one run."

"Terrific, we can practice some more this weekend. How was your math test?"

"I think I did okay. I only left one blank."

"Fine, Kevin. I guess you want to watch television so I'll say good-bye. Talk to you tomorrow."

"Okay, Dad. See ya. Bye."

These routine conversations did nothing to enrich their relationship.

Roger felt he was losing his son. A friend suggested that he establish an area of common interest with Kevin. Since he lived near the beach, Roger came up with the idea of starting a rock and shell collection.

Creating this collection offered father and son many opportunities to spend time together productively. They went on nature walks, spent time at the library researching interesting finds, and visited museums housing varieties of rocks and shells. More importantly, even when Roger and his son were not together, Kevin continued working on his collection and maintained a feeling of his father's presence.

Roger no longer felt it necessary to call his son every night. But when he did call, they had a mutual interest as a basis of their conversations.

Another example of opening new areas of communication was conceived by Renee.

Renee, a painter, saw her children only on weekends and long holidays. Before her divorce, the children had resented her occupation. She had spent long hours in her studio and they had not been allowed in. After her divorce, however, she felt she wanted to give more of herself to her children. Since she was always relaxed when she was painting she decided to involve her children with this part of her life. She began by inviting them to join her at the studio. At first they were slow to respond, since they felt her painting had been one of the reasons for the divorce. Renee, understanding their reluctance, gave them her undivided attention and encouraged them to experiment with her paints. Gradually, the children's interest grew and they all began going to museums together. On weekends they sometimes held outdoor painting sessions. Renee had some of their work framed to take home for their father and stepmother to see. But more important than the paintings were the rewarding times they spent together.

Obviously, not all parents or children are gifted in the same way. Parents who have no particular artistic talent need not feel limited. Collecting stamps, coins, old maps, old books, inkwells, paperweights, army insignia, patches, bottles, old glass—these are just a few of the things a child can develop an interest in and share with a parent.

Tropical fish, for instance, can be much more of a project than just putting goldfish into a bowl. Borrow or buy books on aquarium fish and spend time jointly planning your purchases. You may want to investigate complex ecologies, setting up different kinds of pond environments.

There are many adult education programs for parents and children. Crafts, from model building to woodworking, from needlepoint to macramé, are an ideal area for parents and children to explore. See what is available in your community. Check with the schools, churches, synagogues, and local Ys.

Scouting too provides many new interests and avenues for mutual participation. Under the leadership of a scoutmaster parents can learn along with their sons or daughters. Scouting activities include bicycling, photography, camping, fishing, and many physical fitness programs.

Look for community sports activities. You can devise an exercise routine for you and your child to be done when you are together, and when you are apart.

Regardless of what you do, the important thing is to create your own unique experiences. You do not want to be an observer in your child's life, you want to be a participant. (Watching TV may be a sharing experience but it does not qualify as participating.)

11

Helping Children Cope
with Their Feelings

Communication with children cannot depend solely upon verbal exchanges since it is not always possible for children to express their feelings in words. Children need safe outlets for their aggressions. Creative media are excellent conduits for self-expression. The way in which a child manipulates creative possibilities can be very revealing. While I am not suggesting that parents play amateur psychiatrist, they can nevertheless help a child express his or her feelings through nonverbal media. The artistic quality of their efforts is not nearly as important as the activity itself.

The kneading and pounding of clay, for example, allows for a tremendous release of anxiety. If your child does not know what to do with clay or cannot think of anything to make, offer your suggestions.

You may also ask your children to draw pictures of the things that make them happy and things that make them sad. Children can make collages from magazine pictures and other household materials. Find an appropriate spot in your home to display their efforts.

Writing by your child is another excellent vehicle for your finding out how your child feels. Encourage your children to write stories or poems. Let them choose their own topics. Pay attention to the content. The work will reveal more of their feelings than they are aware of.

For children who are intellectually capable, there are wonderful children's novels that can help a child understand his or her feelings and emotions. Consult your school or public library for books that will be appropriate for your child's age and emotional level.

Involvement in extracurricular activities affords positive avenues for releasing energy. For children whose hostile feelings are at a peak, this may be especially helpful.

Ever since Arlene K.'s divorce her son, Allen, had been hostile and aggressive. He refused to clean up his room, to do his usual chores, and he began having problems with his schoolwork. Despite his mother's efforts to get him to open up she could not get through to him.

She realized that this behavior was his outlet for releasing his aggressive feelings. She found an acceptable release for his aggression quite by accident. A swimming team was forming at the local Y. Allen had always been a good swimmer. It was not difficult to interest him in joining the team. Before long he was involved in swim practice and team competition and was using up so much energy that his aggressiveness was being drawn off. As it diminished it became easier to talk about his real problems. This led to a decrease in his negative behavior. Although the swimming activity was in no way related to his anger and hostility, it helped him to deal with them.

Children's behavior is often designed to conceal their real feelings. For example, Ellen was fifteen. Her parents had been divorced for six months. Her mother had recently started dating. Ellen was always pleasant and polite when introduced by her mother to a man. Her mother often praised her and considered her behavior commendable. She interpreted Ellen's exaggerated politeness as a sign of acceptance. She only heard Ellen's words, "So nice to meet you. My mother told me such nice things about you. Excuse me, please. I know you would like to visit with my mother and I have some homework to do." But Ellen's politeness was only her camouflage for her feeling of resentment toward her mother's dates.

It is not unusual for a parent to misinterpret a child's behavior. How was Ellen's mother to know how she really felt? A parent's instinctive ability to tune into what a child is really saying cannot be learned from a book. But a parent can be alert to any behavior that is exaggerated. Being too good is as much a cry for help as being too bad. When children withdraw, become passive in their outward acceptance of things, their behavior may be welcomed by parents who are weighed down by their own conflicts. A quiet, orderly child is certainly easier to cope with than a child who is disruptive. If Ellen's mother had not been so anxious to interpret Ellen's behavior as a sign of acceptance, she would have recognized the message Ellen was really sending.

It takes a clever parent to discern a child's sincere intention from a calculated maneuver. Carol was a cheerful outgoing ten-year-old who also showed her resentment toward her mother's dating only indirectly. She was most agreeable to the suggestion that her mother's boyfriend, Peter, come over for dinner one evening. Her parents had been divorced for over a year and Peter was only the third man her mother had dated. This was the first time she had invited any man for dinner.

Carol was anxious to help that evening and volunteered to set the table. Her mother gave her very definite instructions about how she wanted it done but Carol paid no attention. Instead of placing Peter at the head of the table, she placed him between herself and her mother. She put the linen napkins aside and instead set out paper napkins. She did not intend to have any other man sit in her father's seat nor did she want her mother to use the silver and crystal that were always used for family celebrations.

When her mother asked Carol why she had not followed instructions, she answered, "I wanted Peter to sit between us so I could talk to him, and I didn't want you to have to wash the good napkins when they got dirty. And," she continued, "these glasses can go in the dishwasher and you do not have to worry about breaking them."

Her mother realized that Carol's elaborate explanation served only as a cover-up for her fears and resentment. She saw that Carol needed more time to accept the situation. She explained to her that no matter who sat in her father's seat, no one would ever take her father's place in Carol's life.

Rebellion comes in many forms. It is much easier to recognize aggressive rebellion in a child than passive resistance. No matter which form the rebellion takes, the child needs help. Recognizing the child's need for help is the first step for the parent. Once the child's cry for help is recognized, the parent must know what to do. One must never ignore the problem and hope that it will go away. Fortunately, most parents realize that this is unlikely. Rarely is a child unhappy and rebellious for no reason. Rarely is a happy child rebellious.

Even inexperienced parents are capable of aiding their child. If, on the other hand, a parent cannot cope with the problem, he or she should seek the guidance of a professional. School counselors, principals, family guidance centers, mental health centers, and social service centers are all inexpensive (sometimes free) places a parent can go to to seek professional advice. It is much wiser to admit that you are having difficulty coping with your child's rebellion and seek outside help than it is to ignore the problem.

Earlier in this chapter you saw a few ways children concealed their real feelings. Passive rebellion is not always easy to recognize. But there are basic behavior patterns that indicate disturbed feelings regardless of how they are camouflaged. Extreme behavior of any kind is a good indication that a child is having a problem. If children are too obedient, too quiet, too meek, too withdrawn, and such behavior was not typical prior to the divorce, the parent should be alerted to a possible problem.

A child's temperament may not permit aggressive displays of rebellion. But exaggerated behavior in the other direction is probably creating tremendous internal tension and unhappiness.

If a child's behavior becomes more withdrawn, he or she may need professional help. Parental intervention alone may not be enough. A parent should try to converse with the child, affording the child an opportunity to voice hostile feelings. Any time you know a child has tried to deceive, by all means tell him or her that you know. Let the child know you understand the reasons for concealing real feelings and that he or she has a right to feel angry sometimes. It is not necessary for the child to hide these feelings. Should the child try to deceive you, do not treat this as intentional lying. It is not a discipline problem. It is a problem that requires patience, understanding, and the warmth of a parent's love.

Let us discuss the aggressively rebellious child. Signs of this type of rebellion are so obvious—most parents are overwhelmed by the chaos such a child creates. Negative aggression can take the form of many kinds of antisocial behavior and destructive acts. Such behavior can be directed toward the parents themselves, toward school situations, or authority figures in general. The results of this type of behavior can permeate every aspect of the child's life. Such children need immediate help or they will eventually destroy their parents and themselves.

There is no point in trying to isolate any one cause for the child's rebellion. There is probably more than one aggravating the situation. It is important to initiate action that will begin to prevent the child from engaging in continuous negative behavior. Children caught up in this type of anger and rebellion usually cannot stop their offensive behavior. The more their behavior provokes punishment and confrontations with the parents, the more rebellious they become. Punishment and parental anger will usually not prevent future outbursts nor will they properly discipline the present one. The poor parent feels ineffective and helpless.

Seek professional help for such a child. Do not hesitate. The sooner you find a good family counseling program the better off everyone will be. A family counselor will provide many helpful ways by which parents can respond to their child's actions. The family must deal with this problem as a unit, involving all members, also including stepparents if any exist.

This is the more extreme form of rebellion. But that does not mean that aggressive rebellion is always so evident and constant. Children may go through periods of aggressive and nonaggressive rebellion that can be adequately helped by skillful, intuitive parental intervention. The purpose of this work is to encourage just this type of parental help.

See also chapter 17, The Co-Parent, for additional information about handling a rebellious child.

12

The Working Mother

It is often necessary for a woman to work after a divorce. The reason is not always financial. Many women simply feel that they cannot continue to stay at home, cut off from other adults. They feel stifled in a world of PTAs, parks, and supermarkets. There may be days at a time when they see no one other than their children or the supermarket clerk. Many women go back to work to alleviate the boredom they feel at home and to meet new people.

If financial reasons have made it necessary for you to go to work, children can be told of this in a way that highlights the fact that both you and your ex-spouse have additional expenses since you now have to maintain two households. You should try not to sound resentful or hostile about the additional financial burdens.

Tell your children what arrangements you will make for them during the hours you will be at work. If you hire a babysitter or a housekeeper, see that they spend some time with the children before you leave them alone together. Do not simply let children come home to find a stranger waiting for them.

You may find that your children become especially demanding of you after you begin to work. Establishing a designated time each day or evening to spend with them will help them feel that you will always make time for them. Your children will be able to look forward to this time with you and it can become treasured moments you will all share. It may even help them to understand that you need time for yourself as well as time for them. Respecting other people's privacy and relinquishing one's own demands are important lessons children must learn. A working mother can use the practicality of her situation to foster this kind of consideration and cooperation in all members of the family. Children can be made to understand that caring and sharing is a mutual thing. Show them that you are willing to give of yourself within reason but you expect their consideration in return. Children will usually respond to reasonable requests on the part of the parent, especially if it is done with tenderness and understanding. There may be times that you are just not up to meeting

[53]

their immediate needs. Instead of taking things out on a child and making him or her feel responsible for your headache or backache, be honest. Tell them you are very tired and a bit out of sorts right now and will probably feel much better in an hour or two. Ask them please to try to understand that right now you are a little short on patience and will appreciate their consideration very much. Parents are often surprised to find that their children will respond with concern and accommodation. If this appeal is not abused and does not become a constant escape on the part of a parent, children can learn to be most cooperative and considerate, especially when they are praised for their efforts when they are successful. Praise and a flattering word from a parent can be a very strong incentive to keep up the admirable behavior. Discipline need not always be heavy-handed.

I want to emphasize the benefit of asking children for their cooperation. Even very young children can be taught to put their things away. If they are old enough they can be asked to help you prepare dinner. It helps a child to mature if there are responsibilities to be assumed, especially when the things they are doing are necessary and not contrived. It gives children an added sense of their own worth to know that they are capable of being useful in a very real and needed way.

A mother who is working out of choice has certain advantages over the mother who is working out of necessity. Although she may be just as tired at the end of a day, she may not feel the emotional pressure of her job as much, and may find it easier to enjoy her children.

If your children feel that they are not being deprived of their share of your time and attention, they will be better able to accept your working. If staying home makes you irritable and frustrated, and working gives you a feeling of satisfaction, there is no reason to stay at home. If you have decided to go back to work and have made the necessary arrangements for care of the children there is no cause to feel guilty.

13

When Fathers Have Custody

It is not unusual today for a father to be awarded full custody of children. In *What About Me?*, there is a discussion of what it is like for children to live with their fathers. Fathers in this situation will enjoy reading that chapter with their children.

When a father has full custody, it is important that the children understand why that arrangement has been made. The particular circumstances and the ages of the children will determine what and how they should be told.

Most of the fathers I spoke to complained of the same problem. They never had enough time for their own personal needs because of all the time they felt duty bound to give to their children. A father is entitled to time for himself. Many fathers are so anxious for the children to be well cared for that they rush home from work to spend every extra minute with their children. It is important to learn to organize priorities in order to have enough time for one's own needs as well as those of the children. A single father should realize that the more fulfilling and well-rounded his life, the better parent he will be.

Some fathers are uneasy about dating. They hesitate to bring a woman home for fear that the children may be resentful or jealous. A man has an advantage here. He does not have to bring a woman to his home unless he chooses to, so he is able to regulate the degree of exposure his children have to the woman he is dating. It is never a good idea to introduce your children to too many different women. But it is wrong to keep children from meeting anyone. Children need to know that their father has friends, female as well as male. It is especially important for a daughter to learn to share her father with female friends. Some daughters have a tendency to take on the role of the missing wife and become overly possessive of their father.

Sometimes fathers try to compensate for the mother's absence by overemphasizing the need for family solidarity. A single father with several children may instill an exaggerated sense of family unity in the children. This can create an overdependency on one another, inhibiting a child's

[55]

ability to grow as an individual. Siblings with divorced parents usually cling to each other for support without any encouragement. They do not really need parental nudging in this direction to bring them together. They will often become far closer than siblings from nondivorced families. A father should not normally interfere with the natural emergence of sibling ties and relationships.

14

Dating

How well a child has accepted his or her parents' divorce has a great deal to do with how willingly he or she will accept their dating. Children who still hope their parents will get together again may harbor deep resentment toward any stranger who they think will interfere.

Many children are reluctant to accept the fact that the parent has begun to make new social contacts. They often regard a new person as an intruder. It is important that a child understand that continuing to see old friends and making new ones is an important part of one's life and that being divorced does not change this. You must constantly assure your child that no one could ever usurp his or her place in your life.

A wise parent will try to understand the apprehension and resentment a child may feel. Suddenly having to share a divorced or divorcing parent with a new person presents much confusion and insecurity to an already shaken child. You should not punish a child who is reluctant to accept a parent's dating. Remember, this is not a discipline problem. The child disturbed by your new social life needs a tolerant, patient parent. Good parent-child communication at this time can establish a rapport that will permeate many parts of your lives.

There is nothing wrong with introducing a child to a potential suitor, but some parents allow their children to become a part of all their social visits and this can be harmful.

I say this for good reason. Most of these new social relationships will probably be very short lived, will end in nothing more than a few casual dates. Children should not take part in all the preliminary aspects of adult dating. You will be meeting many new people. Some of these relationships will be more meaningful than others. At best, it is difficult for adults to cope with the nuances of getting to know a new person. It is unfair to expose children to these difficulties and expect them to participate. Children should not be seriously involved in your relationship until the adults concerned have reached a meaningful level of communication.

This is not to say that children cannot have fun sharing activities with their parent and other adult friends. We all have people with whom we share friendship and with whom we enjoy doing things, simply because there is mutual compatibility. These relationships have no romantic implications and are simply based on friendship. It is important that children see adult communication that is free and open. They will learn more of what it is to be a friend and to have friends by watching the relationships of their parents with other people.

When children are included in an activity, it should be one that is suitable for children. It can be harmful to permit children to be present at activities or events not suitable for their ages. This is particularly important to remember for those occasions when a child is to be included in a parent's date. If the purpose of this outing is for adults and children to get to know each other better, the type of activity chosen is very important. Children will respond better and will be more at ease if they are involved in activities with which they are familiar. When children are forced to participate in activities that are beyond their ken they are often bored and restless. Discipline problems can often occur and children can become very negative. The result is an unpleasant experience for everyone.

Before planning a date that is to include a child, consider the age of the child, the sex of the child, and the suitability of where you are going and what you are doing. Wise planning will usually result in a greater rapport between adult and child.

Just as it is important to you that your children like the person you are dating, it is natural for you to want his or her children to like you. Do not be disappointed if an instant rapport does not develop. Consider the children's feelings and try to understand the problems they may have accepting you. A child who is unresponsive or even hostile toward you at first often responds to patience. Your relationship will depend on what you put into it. You can never get a child to like you by using bribery. Adults often try to buy the friendship and goodwill of children. No matter how well intentioned this is, the adult may find himself cast in the role of Santa Claus. You may discover that the demands of a child are endless. Nothing you do will be enough. Eventually you begin to resent the very child you are trying so hard to cultivate. You cannot force your attention on a child who is not ready to accept you.

Here is where good common sense and discretion on your part are essential. Timing is most important in successfully advancing a new relationship with a child.

15

Living with Someone to Whom
You Are Not Married

One of the most controversial areas of single parent life is that of living with someone of the opposite sex while remaining unmarried. There is little in the way of research that one can point to in discussing the ramifications of these living arrangements. Parents are pretty much on their own in determining what is right for themselves and for their children.

Parents, just like everyone else, have a right to their own private lives. They also, however, have a responsibility to their children. Most parents whose children live at home refrain from frequently changing bed partners. A man or woman may have any number of serious romances, however, before he or she is ready to remarry.

Many divorced people, having been disappointed, are unwilling to consider marriage without first living with the partner-to-be. Many enter into a premarital arrangement in the belief that they will soon marry. This may turn out to be a very positive relationship for everyone, having little if any effect on the children after the couple is married. But, if there is more than a reasonable doubt of the prospect of marriage, entering into this kind of an arrangement is, I believe, unfair to children. The concern is not with how well everything may appear to be going when you are all together but with what will happen if you break up. The morality of such an arrangement is not at issue in this book. The only concern is with the effect it may have upon the children.

When children are involved, their welfare must be carefully considered. Children can be left with deep emotional scars when people to whom they form attachments suddenly disappear. They have already endured the trauma of witnessing the departure of a parent. The repetition of this experience can only be even more painful.

I am not suggesting that a sleep-over guest on occasion is wrong. Quite the contrary. Children may enjoy the novelty of having someone special spending the night in their home. But that is just what it should be, a novelty. I am not recommending a sleep-over guest when the only available bed is your own. Discretion and decorum are necessary. Children learn from what they see, not just what they are told.

Many parents think that because their children are young they do not know what is going on. Bear in mind that while they may not fully understand they know *something* is going on, and their feelings toward their parent and toward sex can be strongly affected by this in later years. Whether one realizes it or not, children are very much involved with someone their parent is living with, whether married or not.

In order to get the child's point of view on such living arrangements I interviewed fifty children between the ages of eight and sixteen. Many factors were involved in determining the child's reaction. The age of the child, the sex of the child, the child's relationship to the parent and to the outsider living with the parent, how long the parent had been divorced, whether the other parent had remarried, the kind of life they had before their parent started living with someone, how much the child understood about what goes on in an adult's bed—all these things had tremendous bearing upon a child's attitude toward his or her parent living with someone. Parental permissiveness toward sex was also reflected in the child's reactions.

Adolescent boys seemed most resentful of their mothers who lived with men to whom they were not married. They felt that they were being deprived of their mother by men who did not have a right to share her. "After all," said one twelve-year-old boy, "he's not married to my mother, he's only sleeping with her." This boy admitted liking his mother's lover but felt that the man did not have the same rights that his father had when his parents were still married. The boy did not have any objections to his mother marrying this man. But he did not like the idea of her living with him. When I asked him if he had ever said anything to his mother, he told me that he had not. It was none of his business and his mother would do what she wanted to.

A fourteen-year-old boy living with his father and his father's girl friend thought that it was really "groovy." He told me that things were much better around the house since she was living there. Their food was better and everything seemed to be more the way it was when his mother was around. He liked Carol very much and really wanted his father to marry her. But he did not know if this was a good idea because his mother was not married yet and he did not want to see her hurt anymore.

[60]

Eight-year-old Pamela liked the man her mother was living with very much. He was very nice to Pamela and did many things with her that her mother would not do. Besides, she told me, her mother was much better to Pamela since he had moved in. Before that her mother was very grumpy much of the time. She was only pleasant when Peter was staying over. Now she was nice and more fun to be with all the time. Pamela did not really care whether they got married or not and did not seem to be thinking about this at all. She only hoped that Peter would not go away because everything was so lovely when he was there.

Fifteen-year-old Margarite did not like the woman who had moved in with her, her brother, and her father. She said the woman was mean and made Margarite do all kinds of things around the house. The woman was only nice when father was home. She told me that if her father married this woman, she would run away. But she knew that her father would never marry this woman because he was never going to marry anyone again. Margarite's mother had left them four years earlier for a man she was having an affair with. Although she was still not married to him, she was living with that man. She came to visit her children often enough but rarely did she take them to her own home. The children knew the man she was living with but very rarely saw him. Margarite did not seem to care whether either of her parents got married. She was certain that she was not going to get married when she grew up.

Fourteen-year-old Monica liked the man her mother was living with very much. But she had to admit that she was embarrassed sometimes when her girl friends came over and saw that her mother was living with Larry and that they were not married. Not that it really matters, she said, but there are times that I wish they were really married. Monica told me that sometimes, when she is in her bed at night, she thinks about her mother in there with Larry and it makes her angry. She did not know why she got angry but she just did. She never thought about it when her father was in bed with her mother but she thought about it a lot since Larry moved in. She also wondered how her father felt about it. He never said anything but she really did not think he liked it. Sometimes she felt sorry for her father because he was all alone. In spite of her mixed feelings, she really wished that, if Larry were going to stay, he would marry her mother.

Eleven-year-old Adam was tired of living with just his mother and his older brother. He wished that his mother would find someone to live with so that she would not be so unhappy all the time. She really got unhappy when his father married again. Ever since his father remarried, his mother looked sad. She tried to be cheerful and she tried making believe that she was happy but Adam could see how unhappy she was. Adam thinks that she really misses his father and he knows that if she had someone else instead of his father she would be all right. His older brother told him that was what the trouble was. To Adam, living with a man or being married to him was the same thing. He just wanted to see a man living with them.

These cases demonstrate the diversity of situation and response. No two children reacted exactly the same way. The older children seemed to have more definite feelings than the younger ones. Obviously they were capable of understanding much more of what was going on. The only thing that was true for all of them was that they were all deeply affected by the emotional arrangements of their households.

16

The Joy of Remarriage

Since 40 percent of all marriages end in divorce, it is not surprising to learn that remarriage too is on the rise. Statistics tell us that four out of every five divorced parents remarry. I find this comforting to note insofar as it does assure the continuation of marriage as an institution and as the core of our family relationships. What people are objecting to and seeking to change is the particular mate and not the state of marriage.

Sadly, however, 44 percent of these remarriages also end in divorce. Why?

It seems pointless to begin any discussions of remarriage without first talking about marriage and your first marriage in particular.

How does one evaluate the collapse of a marriage? Often divorce is not only the dissolution of a marriage, it is also the rejection of a life-style that was unfulfilling and unrewarding. For many adults unhappiness with their spouses was symptomatic of the underlying displeasure with their entire lives, leaving them with feelings of frustration and futility. After a divorce many people spend sleepless nights asking themselves, "What went wrong? Why did it happen? Could we have prevented it? How much of it was my fault?" In this state of mind it is usually impossible to do more than ask oneself questions. Before long some individuals find themselves involved in a new marriage that proves to be just as unsatisfying as the one just dissolved. They have leaped head first into a second marriage to assuage their pain, never understanding what went wrong the first time.

Paradoxically, for some a divorce is the catalyst that fosters growth and self-awareness. Such a person, it is hoped, will be able to approach a second marriage with more insight and a deeper awareness of what they can bring to the marriage and what they may expect in return.

Some may enter a second marriage for financial reasons. A marriage based on finances is no substitute for a marriage built on love. Money alone can neither build nor destroy a good marriage. A marriage can be a good one even when there are serious money problems. Many partners endure great financial hardships and survive simply because they have each other.

[63]

All this paints a dismal picture for the success of remarriage. But it is necessary to be aware of problems so that one can attempt to avoid them. I for one am very optimistic about the success of remarriage.

I call this chapter "The Joy of Remarriage" because most people who do remarry have every chance of finding the happiness they are hoping for. The second time can have many advantages over the first time, especially if we are wiser and better able to cope with the realities of marriage. Most people who have been married before are no longer naïve. Their fantasies and romantic illusions no longer exist. If they have learned from their mistakes and have matured, they can enter into a stable and rewarding relationship. Divorce need not be a tragic end when it opens up the way to a new and successful life with someone else.

Fortunately most people who get a divorce have not lost the need or capacity to love someone else. They often find they are capable of sharing a deeper, more meaningful love than ever before. The aftermath of a divorce can lead to many changes in one's personality. Overcoming the trauma forges new strength and independence. Many people find that they emerge from the turmoil of their divorce far more capable than they ever believed they could be. Consequently, the quality of life they can share with someone else will be much richer.

Thus, remarriage can truly provide the joy that they expected in their original marriage. But it would be unfair to paint this rosy picture without also discussing the problems remarriage can bring.

In chapter 14 on dating you noted the importance of keeping children out of transitory relationships. But children do have a place in a growing relationship, especially one that may be leading to marriage. Children must feel they are part of your future, part of the new life you are building. If both parents have children they should be brought together frequently. Especially if they will soon be living together. The things you do together now will set the pace for the family's future.

Anticipating the problems or complications surrounding your re-marriage is important. When possible such matters should be dealt with prior to the marriage. Of course this is not always possible but one should make the effort.

If the number of immediate problems caused by your remarriage is great, it is possible that these reflect basic underlying problems. When family relationships have been going smoothly prior to remarriage, it is unlikely that many meaningful problems will develop suddenly.

It is fairly common for newly divorced parents to make one mistake that often leads to serious problems at the time of remarriage. Some parents refuse to acknowledge the possibility that they may ever remarry, assuring their children that this will never happen. The bitterness and cynicism that such an attitude conveys can do a great deal of harm. The children's attitude toward marriage and a stable family life can be severely affected.

Even more serious is the effect on the children when ultimately the parent does want to marry. The children, already severely upset by the breakup of the home, are now faced with an unreliable parent about to create a similar situation. It is never a good idea to be overemphatic about anything in life that you cannot accurately predict. Even if you believe that you will never marry again it is still wiser to keep these feelings to yourself.

Chapters 10, 11, and 12 in *What About Me?* should help you understand some of the apprehensions children may have regarding a parent's remarriage and some very legitimate fears and anxieties. It is important that their questions and fears be dealt with tactfully and understandingly. It is preferable to have your new spouse add whatever reassurance he or she can offer as well. His or her willingness to accept the child in spite of whatever apprehensions are present will go a long way to reduce the child's fears.

17

The Co-Parent (Stepparent)

A new type of family unit will have a significant impact on society in the future. This new family unit can be called the multiparent family, consisting of more than two parents who function as co-parents for the same children.

By the time you consider remarriage your children should not be strangers to your prospective mate.

All that has been said regarding the parent-child relationship at the time of a divorce pertains to the stepparent-child relationship. Just as an adult brings the sum total of his being—physical, spiritual, moral, emotional—to a new marriage, so does a child. The nature of a child's relationship with each of his or her natural parents will determine the nature of the relationship that will develop between a child and a stepparent. There is no way of detaching the child from his or her past. Nor should you ever want to. Children in this situation must adapt to a change. They must accept the authority of a new person in the role of a parent, and, at the same time, recognize the authority of their natural parents.

The age of a child when a parent enters into a marriage is significant. It often appears that younger children show fewer signs of being disturbed than do older children. But this can be very deceptive. Often younger children cannot express themselves as positively and are not able to give voice to their real feelings. Very young children of three or four years can be so confused that they cannot understand the reality of the new marriage.

The younger child's passive acceptance of a situation over which he or she has no control can be very misleading. At some point younger children will have to decide how they really feel about living with their biological mother or father, and a stepparent. They cannot yet understand the further implications of the new marriage and only react to it in terms of the way it affects them. Young children are somewhat egocentric in their acceptance of anything. As long as the new environment does not appear to disrupt their own good style of life it cannot be so very bad.

A very young child will not have much difficulty accepting a stepparent who is warm and loving. In time he or she will probably begin to view the stepparent in very much the same way as the biological parent. Young children may even grow to be closer to the stepparent than to the natural parent because of the time they spend with the former.

How a stepparent-stepchild relationship progresses is so complex and varied that this book cannot attempt to explore its intricacies. All I can hope to do here is highlight the major considerations with which a parent should initially be concerned, and those things that will make the new marriage and the parent-child adjustment more successful.

Perhaps the most important element in successful second marriage family relations is that the partners actively support each other. The ideal situation is one in which all the adults concerned, original parents as well as stepparents, can agree on the role each of them will take. In this way they accept each other as co-parents of the same children.

When one remarries, one must not forget that the ex-spouse still retains all the same rights as before regarding the children. Even if your children are living with you, your ex-spouse still has the right, unless otherwise decreed by a court, to be involved with every aspect of his or her children's lives. It is very difficult for some people to accept this fact after they remarry. They should never refuse permission to an ex-spouse to see the children.

A child needs to know and understand both his natural parents. Only in extreme circumstances might a child be better off not exposed to the influence of one natural parent. But this is the rare case.

Regardless of your feelings toward your ex-spouse you should remember that your children still have a right to their own opinions and to return the warmth and love of both parents. In order to achieve a healthy, happy environment, a delicate balance must be maintained by all adults involved. Natural parents and stepparents must work as a team for the well-being of the children. The children are reassured and their tension is dissipated when they see the adults in their family cooperating.

How often the children see the parent with whom they are not living, and how actively involved this parent is in the raising of the children, will have a great deal to do with the role the stepparent assumes. In a case when distance or other causes make it impossible for the natural parent to participate in the child's life, a stepparent will have to assume more authority and responsibility.

It is not unusual for an ex-spouse whose children are living with a stepparent to have ambivalent feelings. He or she may feel undermined by the new parent and feel a need to compete for the children's affection. In addition, the absent parent may be plagued by feelings of guilt and remorse that some other person is living with the children instead of their living with him or her.

I would never attempt to tell a parent who feels this way how wrong he or she is, because this is virtually a universal reaction for the absent parent who really cares about the children.

It is best to try to help this parent gain a greater sense of security about his or her relationship with the children. Only then will the absent parent be less likely to feel threatened by the new parent and know that the children still love him or her. A secure parent will be able to accept the new stepparent with less ambivalence and, we hope, reach a mutual agreement as to the role they will both share in raising the children.

The same holds true for a wise stepparent who must remember that the children are new to him or her. A healthy relationship cannot be forced prematurely. In most instances a stepparent should never attempt to take the place of a child's natural parent. The stepparent role often can begin as one of a friend who is sincerely concerned about the feelings and welfare of the children. Many stepparents make the mistake of wanting to show deep love and affection for their new children almost immediately. They are disappointed when this sincere affection is not accepted by the child or returned by the child. Children should not be forced to respond with simulated affection and feelings they might not yet have. Some children take considerable time before they can feel secure enough to be able to respond with proper affection for both natural and stepparents. Many children feel that they are being disloyal to their biological parents if they begin to like their stepparents. Never, under any circumstances, should a stepparent speak negatively about the children's natural parent, nor should he or she allow any such conversations to take place in the children's presence.

The role of a stepmother is particularly precarious. A woman who gains children along with a new husband must learn to be a diplomat, especially if she has children of her own. Since most husbands will probably be away from home most of the day, the job of cementing the new family together will be up to the stepmother.

The attitude a stepmother shows toward her new children, particularly if her own children are there as a measuring rod, can determine the success of her new family. Common sense dictates that high in the order of priorities are fairness and equal treatment for all the children. Even if this goal seems impossible, you must work very hard toward it. The most common problem parents have with siblings of the same parentage is jealousy over parental attention. When stepsiblings are involved, the problem is aggravated. Remember that rivalry over parental attention and affection is normal and has to be dealt with accordingly. When stepparents are present there is the risk of an exaggerated sense of jealousy and feelings of unjust persecution on the part of one child or another.

A stepmother is particularly vulnerable because the children will vie for her attention and affection constantly. Stepchildren, especially those of elementary school age, will constantly compare her treatment of them to her treatment of her own children. A wise stepmother will make sure to keep a fair balance.

If children are living with a stepmother instead of their natural mother there are probably very good reasons. Even though it is becoming more usual to see fathers awarded custody of the children, it is still the mother who is usually given preference. Often when the children are not living with their natural mother it is by mutual agreement of both spouses. A mother who has made this decision is usually not resentful of a stepmother. Of course if this arrangement has been forced upon the mother for one reason or another, there will probably be many problems between the two women. Whenever possible, a stepmother should try to gain the cooperation of the children's natural mother and work as a team with her. Both are co-parents of the children. A good working rapport between the two women will be most beneficial to the children. Often the first move must come from the stepmother.

There are fewer complications with a stepmother when the children do not live with her. A smart woman will befriend her husband's children and have an open door policy toward them. They should be made to feel that they are not unwelcome in her home but very much wanted there. She should understand that, at the beginning, they might show some resentment toward her. In this case she should not try to force things. The children's attitude toward her may reflect that of their mother to some degree. It is really up to the father to pave the way for his children's acceptance of his new wife. If serious problems are caused by his ex-wife, he should try to discuss matters (if possible) with her and try to work out a practical solution. And to repeat: Never should the new wife belittle the children's natural mother or speak badly about her in front of the children.

Sometimes it is difficult for children to accept the attention and affection their father may give his new wife. That is especially true if they see their own mother unhappy much of the time. In the beginning stepparents should be discreet about their display of affection toward each other in front of the children.

When one set of children in a second marriage lives elsewhere, they should be made to feel that they are always welcome in your home. If possible, a room should be set aside for them to use. Try to include them in as many family activities as possible. They should be assured that you still want them and care very much about them even though you may be living with someone else's children. A parent should be sure to include his or her children in as many aspects of the new life as possible. Even if the children resist, do not stop trying. In time they will probably accept your overtures if you are sincere, tactful, and do not pressure them.

Children are often confused about the name for a new parent. The term "stepfather" or "stepmother" often carries a negative connotation for young children who are familiar with the wicked stepmother in *Cinderella*. This problem is discussed in *What About Me?* You should read this section with your children. Children should not be forced to call a new parent "mother" or "father" or "mommy" or "daddy" unless they are comfortable with these terms.

Both the parents with whom the children are living, regardless of whether one is a stepparent, should use their judgment and discretion in raising the children. A stepfather who has assumed the responsibility of partially or fully supporting his new family should play a significant role in the conduct of the household and the family in it. A stepmother who has assumed the responsibility of making a home for her new children should definitely participate in setting standards for the children and seeing that they are adhered to. When a stepfather deems it necessary to administer punishment, the mother should not interfere. She should be supportive of her husband's actions. When a stepmother finds it necessary to reprimand a child she should get the same support from her husband. If there is disagreement between adults, it should be aired at a time when the children are not present.

Parents in a second marriage may make the mistake of trying to appease a child while undermining each other's authority. If children sense a division among the parents, they frequently use it to their own advantage. Children quickly master the art of pitting parent against stepparent. If a child is successful in such maneuvering, he or she can jeopardize the marriage.

Although stepparents may appear to have more problems than natural parents, this is really not so. Good parents and good stepparents will be successful in the rearing of the children. A weak or negligent natural parent will fare no better as a stepparent. Common sense, love, understanding, and principles are necessary in any parent-child relationship.

Although there is no set formula for successful parenting or stepparenting, here is a sketch of suggested types of encounters and behaviors to avoid and to foster.

Attempts at giving real compliments to a stepchild can go very far in developing friendly relations. But make sure your praise is for a sincere cause and not artificial. Children usually know when their deeds are praiseworthy and when they are being patronized.

If children make the first overtures by way of engaging in a conversation or suggesting an activity, take advantage of it. Even if it may sometimes mean stopping what you are presently doing to join them or to listen to them. Be as congenial as possible without exaggerating your response.

Never be pushy but try to tune into moments when you may be able to initiate activities wit the child. Make sure never to interfere with the child's activity time with his or her natural parent on a visiting day.

Let the child know that you respect his or her absent parent and understand how much he or she loves this parent and probably misses him or her very much. Make it very clear to the child that you do not want to replace this parent. You want to be a good friend and share whatever you can with the child in addition to what they share with their absent parent.

Avoid disagreements over the children or over personal matters with your spouse in front of the children.

Try to avoid unpleasant scenes or confrontations over discipline with the child himself or herself. You will gain nothing from a head-on clash with a negative, rebellious child. This child may be intentionally offensive to you and try to provoke arguments from you as a way of justifying his or her resentment of you. Obviously this child is having a problem accepting you as a stepparent. Continued confrontations between you will only worsen the situation. It is much wiser for you to walk away and avoid the child's presence at times when you feel you cannot tolerate his or her behavior than to react in a harsh and punitive manner. Although walking away is not a solution, it will prevent further complication for the moment, allowing you time to seek professional guidance and help for a chronic problem such as this.

Obviously a stepparent should exercise more control over his or her temper and make every effort to avoid losing his or her temper with a stepchild.

18

How to Answer Your
Child's Accusations

When children say they are misunderstood and constantly mistreated, that they have the worst father or mother in the world, that they hate you and wish they had someone else for a parent, you will ask yourself where you went wrong. Is the divorce to blame?

It is not unusual for children occasionally to behave this way, but natural parents take it all in stride. With their almost inevitable guilt feelings, however, divorced parents are far more vulnerable to accusations that everything that goes wrong for children is the fault of parent and stepparent. This situation can create serious family problems.

Parents should be prepared to handle such accusations without being intimidated. Read some of the suggested books on child development. It is important not to confuse what is part of normal child development with what is caused by a divorce.

A parent who allows himself or herself to believe that the divorce alone is responsible for a child's problems is soon at the mercy of the child. Effectiveness as a parent will shortly disappear.

No one can say that raising children is easy whether one is married, divorced, or remarried. When your child hits you with "I wish I had parents who really cared about me, who didn't get a divorce," or "I hate you and I'm glad you got divorced," do not retort with attacks on the child's current behavior or role in the divorce. One way to answer angry, unhappy children is to say that as bad as they may think you are, you are still the only mother or father they have got. And in spite of anything they may think, you still love them very much and are doing your utmost to be the best parent you can. Add that you are truly sorry that they are unhappy and you hope that when they feel better you can both talk about what is really troubling them.

This type of answer will be more disarming than an angry, sarcastic response. Letting your children see that you are in control of the situation is reassuring and may encourage them to talk to you about their deepest feelings.

Parents should try to remember that their children will eventually mature. With this maturity will come the realization that their parents' divorce was not necessarily the cause of all their problems.

[73]

19

Special Problems

Alcoholism, Drug Addiction, Mental Illness

If alcoholism, drug addiction, or mental illness is the cause of a divorce, it is imperative that the children understand that the afflicted parent is ill. The child should be told if the parent is to be hospitalized. If medical doctors or psychiatrists are involved in the treatment, do not hesitate to ask them for advice about what and how much to tell the children. If the ill parent is not yet receiving or even seeking treatment, there are several organizations that offer help to families. You can find out which organizations may be available in your community by calling the local chamber of commerce or the social service or mental health department in your community hospital.

In such situations the afflicted parent has probably been functioning in a disoriented way for some time. A child may wonder whether his or her parent's affliction is inherited. They will be curious about why or how it happened. When violent or disoriented behavior occurs, children may become fearful and resentful of their ill parent. To a child who has witnessed scenes that were unpleasant or frightening, a divorce may come as a blessing since it removes the troublesome parent from his or her daily life. A child may be burdened by inner conflicts and guilt as a result of his or her resentment and the desire to be rid of that parent. Children should, of course, be encouraged to talk about what is troubling them and should be told as much of the truth as their level of maturity allows.

Perhaps you might voice your own sense of relief at no longer having to live with the ill parent. Tell children that it is understandable to feel this way. It is important to stress that the ill parent needs professional help, which neither you nor your child is equipped to offer. Assure your child that he or she is in no way to blame for the other parent's affliction.

Most parents with such illnesses do love their children but are often unable to show their love and concern. Their illness may cause them to inflict many hurts upon a child, causing him to doubt that the parent loves or cares for him at all. It is helpful to make a distinction between the affliction and the behavior linked to it, and the unintentional hurt that behavior may cause.

Children need the understanding and encouragement of the remaining parent if they are to learn to accept the affected parent's illness. Remember that you have divorced this parent and therefore probably do not retain feelings of love. But children cannot divorce a mother or father, and may still love your former spouse in spite of everything. Try to help them cope with the hurt that this love will cause them.

In this situation responsibility rests heavily upon the parent who has custody. In many instances you will be making unilateral decisions regarding the welfare of the children. If one feels overburdened or incapable of handling this dual role, he or she should seek the advice of a professional counselor. There is probably a service available in the hospital or institution in which your ex-spouse is a patient.

When a Judge Must Decide Custody

When a custody suit is instituted it is indeed unfortunate for all concerned. Any conscientious attorney will do everything possible to try to have things settled outside a courtroom. When children have to rebound from one parent to the other, the harm to the child's psyche will usually be great and long-lasting.

If a judge must decide custody, neither parent is really the victor. You may win the battles but will lose the child to all sorts of anxieties and problems. Regardless of which parent wins, the children have been through great emotional traumas as a result of the courtroom proceedings. Even when children are kept outside the courtroom, and shielded from the proceedings inside, they will still reflect tensions and anxieties. Sensitive, intelligent children cannot help but realize that they are the reason for the controversy. The best advice to parents involved in a custody suit is: Think again. Talk some more. Try to resolve your differences at a lawyer's table outside the courtroom. At all costs, forego ego and the need for revenge. Your children will be the real beneficiaries.

When Parents Continue to Disagree

Parents who continue to have ugly arguments and harsh disagreements while their children are present are destroying not only their own lives but those of their children as well. It is very harmful for children to see constant bickering and friction between their estranged parents.

Such parental behavior leaves children insecure and disoriented regarding all adult relationships. It undermines children's respect for their parents and makes them feel both angry and sad. Worst of all, it leaves them with no one they can look up to and try to emulate as a respected model.

Children should never be subjected to the pressure of having to take sides with one parent or another. They should never be forced to carry tales of what one or the other parent does. Children were not meant to be spies for jealous, immature parents.

In *What About Me?* this problem is discussed very openly. Children whose parents are behaving this way are advised to seek the help of another adult. Very often parents who are behaving this way are not really in control of their actions or their lives. In such cases the parents may need the intervention of a friend or another adult whose judgment they value to help them recognize how destructive their behavior is.

A Parent Who Does Not Love a Child

A parent who does not love his or her own child is a person to be pitied. This parent has problems far greater than simply that of a divorce. The effect on the child is incalculable.

It is very important that a child be helped to understand that in this situation there is nothing wrong with him or her and that he or she is not to be blamed for the inadequacies of the parent. Children must be assured and reassured many times over that they are lovable and worthwhile persons. Prove it by showing them the people who *do* love them. You can invoke all the family members who love and want the children.

In the case in which one parent has abandoned both the child and the spouse, the remaining parent finds himself or herself in a quandary. The parent does not know whether to shield the child from the truth or risk the traumatic effect of letting the child know that this departed parent has no feelings for either spouse or child. It is never easy to tell a child that he or she is not loved or wanted by a parent but this truth, no matter how painful, must be told. One must avoid telling it harshly, abruptly, or with evident resentment. There are gentle ways to explain to a child that this is the situation and that the child is not responsible for the faults of a parent.

It is wrong to try to shield children by giving them fictitious explanations of where their missing parent has gone. It is wrong to keep telling a child how much they are loved by a parent who never comes to see them or who never telephones them, or does not show any interest.

Children's concepts of what love is all about come from the relationships they share in the home, and what they have seen their parents do. Being told one thing but being treated in quite another manner (see the example in *What About Me?* i.e., the story about the neglect of Shadow, the dog) can seriously distort a child's concept of what love really is. Children must learn that love is more than just rhetoric.

Any parent who must cope with this problem will benefit from reading this corresponding section in *What About Me?*

Conclusion

What Does It All Add Up To?

Can a family that has endured divorce still be a caring and close-knit family? Many parents fear that their divorce will turn their children away from them and reduce the importance of the family unit.

After a divorce, even though your family does not exist as a traditional whole any longer, it is still a family.

A well-loved child, secure in his or her parents' affections, will not be easily hurt, and a solid parent-child tie is not easily broken. The divorce may temporarily upset the children but when all the basic relationships are healthy the damage need not be all-encompassing or permanent. The free flow of communication between parents and children is a precious and important factor in building confidence for the future.

Adversity has been known to strengthen and bring families together. Many siblings will turn to one another for comfort and reassurance during the early days of the divorce. They may even exaggerate their relationship to each of their parents as a substitute for the full family unit that no longer exists. The absence of the bond between parents need not interfere with the sibling bonds, nor with the parent-child bond.

Gradually children can come to recognize that the *bonds* that unite them as a family are much deeper than the mere combined *presence* of mother and father. After all, what happens when a parent dies? Families that were close and caring before continue the same way.

Family relationships that are built on mutual trust and confidence are difficult to destroy. The fabric of family bonds is strong and permanent, woven of many threads.

Divorced parents, like all parents, are human enough to make mistakes, but also like all parents, they can provide the love to make their children secure human beings, capable of strong family ties. Parents can be reasonably sure that their demonstrated feelings for their children, and the family life they will continue to share, can more than balance any errors they may commit. Your dissolved marriage is a mistake two very human people made. The children of this union were not a mistake. The love and devotion of parents to their children can continue outside the framework of a marriage.

[78]

Conclusion

When parents continue to place a high value on the welfare of each family member, they are setting an example for their children. Kinship with children may become more powerful than the separation of parents. Parents who continue to respect each other and to participate in their children's lives are placing a high value on the importance of family ties. The fact that they are no longer living together in marriage does not have to reduce the beauty of kinship their union created.

Children can still turn to their parents for the protection and encouragement that all children need. The family heritage that will pass from one generation to the next can still be an integral part of children's lives. Family celebrations and special occasions, holidays, birthdays, can remain important milestones in the continuing development of children. The underlying bonds that make a family feel love and concern can remain in spite of a divorce.

Epilogue

Children have a right to reach maturity as trusting adults, uncynical, and with as much optimism as life can offer them. Parents should keep this in mind when sorting out the pieces of a broken marriage.

A divorce need not be a catastrophic event that throws children into the toils of despair. When parents can come to terms with themselves and their lives they are better able to guide their children through all the detours that may arise. Detours should simply mean that it may be a little more difficult to get where we are going; but with the proper actions and sensitivities we can still arrive at our destination.

Children have tremendous stamina and are resilient when the adults upon whom they depend live up to their expectations. Remember, children are not young forever. They will be the parents of tomorrow.

Do not let the bitterness and hurt of divorce be the only legacy they receive.

Bibliography

Child Development

Adams, James. *Understanding Adolescence.* Boston: Allyn & Bacon, 1968.

Ahere, Giles Nell. *Teenage Living.* Boston: Houghton Mifflin, 1960.

Cole, Luella. *Psychology of Adolescence.* New York: Holt, Rinehart & Winston, 1964.

Crow, Lester D. *Adolescent Development and Adjustment.* New York: McGraw-Hill, 1965.

Despert, Juliette. *Children of Divorce.* Dolphin books, 1962.

Douglas, James William B. *Children under Five.* London: Allen & Unwin, 1958.

*Fraiberg, Selma. *The Magic Years.* New York: Scribner's, 1959.

Fremon, Suzan Strait. *Children and Their Parents.* New York: Harper & Row, 1968.

Furfey, Paul Hanly. *The Growing Boy.* New York: Macmillan, 1930.

Gallagher, James Roswell. *Emotional Problems of Adolescents.* New York: Oxford Community Press, 1958.

Garrison, Karl Claudius. *Psychology of Adolescence.* Englewood Cliffs, New Jersey: Prentice-Hall, 1956.

*Gesell, Arnold, et al. *Youth: Years from Ten to Sixteen.* New York: Harper & Row, 1956.

*Ginott, Haim. *Between Parent and Child.* New York: Macmillan, 1965.

Goodman, David. *A Parent's Guide to the Emotional Needs of Children.* New York: Hawthorn Books, 1959.

Hadfield, James Arthur. *Childhood and Adolescence.* Baltimore: Penguin Books, 1962.

Konopha, Gisila. *Young Girls—A Portrait of Adolescence.* Englewood Cliffs, New Jersey: Prentice-Hall, 1976.

Liebman, Samuel. *Emotional Forces in the Family.* Philadelphia: Lippincott, 1959.

Moser, Clarence. *Understanding Boys.* New York: New York University Press, 1953.

*Smith, Sally Lieberman. *Nobody Said It's Easy.* New York: Macmillan, 1965.

Spitz, Renee. *The First Year of Life.* New York: International University Press, 1965.

Symonds, Percival Mallon. *The Psychology of Parent-Child Relationships.* New York: Appleton Century, 1939.

*Easiest books for the lay person to read.